WITHDRAWN

# ASIAN CIVILIZATION

L. A. Peter Gosling and William D. Schorger
*General Editors*

This series of interdisciplinary readings is designed to introduce the western reader to the distinctive components of Asian civilization—social order, political institutions, economic problems, and cultural milieu. Each set of paired volumes contrasts ancient and modern subjects; ageless tradition has been balanced by recent analysis to reveal historical continuity amid the unprecedented change occurring in Asia today.

**O. L. Chavarria-Aguilar,** editor of this volume in the Asian Civilization series, is Professor of Linguistics at the University of Michigan where he teaches Sanskrit and Hindi, in addition to general linguistics, and lectures on India. He is active in the work of the Center for Southern Asian Studies of the University of Michigan. Professor Chavarria-Aguilar, a graduate of the University of California at Berkeley, received his Ph.D. from the University of Pennsylvania.

FORTHCOMING TITLES

*Modern China* edited by Albert Feuerwerker

*Modern Southeast Asia* edited by John Bastin

*The Modern Near East* edited by William D. Schorger

*The Great Tradition of Asia* edited by L. A. Peter Gosling

*Modern Japan* edited by Roger F. Hackett

*Traditional Japan* edited by Richard K. Beardsley

# TRADITIONAL INDIA

Edited by

O. L. Chavarria-Aguilar

Prentice-Hall, Inc. A SPECTRUM BOOK *Englewood Cliffs, N.J.*

*Library of Congress Catalog Card Number: 64-21958*

Printed in the United States of America—C. P 92603, C 92604

# CONTENTS

# INTRODUCTION

## O. L. Chavarria-Aguilar

India, with China, is one of the oldest *continuous* civilizations of which we have knowledge and record—and the record is an almost staggeringly extensive one. It is a record which, beginning with the Vedas, takes us from the second millennium B.C.—and perhaps beyond—without significant interruption through to the present day. But we shall stop long before the present, since our concern is with the traditional period, with that period in which the characteristic features of Indian culture as we know it were being molded.

The literary sources of our knowledge of ancient India are incredibly vast and represent almost every area of knowledge and human intellectual endeavor save one—unfortunately, a very important one: history. The ancient Indians developed to a high degree of sophistication the areas of mathematics, astronomy, grammar, music, political theory, and, above all, religion and philosophy—each with an extensive literature of its own; but a more unhistorical people would be difficult to find. Thus the history of ancient India is not an Indian history in the sense that the Indians themselves wrote it as such; rather, it is a reconstruction from the literatures just mentioned, with felicitous addition and corroborations from Greek sources and from, among others, the accounts of Chinese Buddhist pilgrims. Note, for instance, in the section on industry, trade, and currency that the Indian sources most frequently cited (other than the *Arthaśāstra,* an economic-political treatise) are the *Jātakas,* which are part of the canon of Buddhism. That is, much of our knowledge of the history of the traditional Indian period comes to us from sources that are not strictly history.

Yet, for the period with which we are concerned, the country and its achievements emerge more clearly in outline and perspective than its people. This period of concern covers, say, the last six or so centuries of the pre-Christian era, roughly the Epic Period (see "History of Indian Thought"). It is a dynamic and fascinating period of change and movement, of religious and social innovation, of speculation and appraisal. Above all, it is the period in which the matrix of Indian culture was being given its characteristic form.

The aspect of traditional India that comes out most clearly and looms largest is the religious and philosophical. "Religio-philosophical" might be the better term (were it not so clumsy and unesthetic) for the two in India are never clearly separable. Its literature is by far the most extensive, and it is surely in this area that the world is most deeply indebted to India. The mathematician may thank India for the concept of zero; the linguist may remain in awe of the system of Pāṇini and his commentators; Machiavelli might have found a kindred soul in Kauṭilya, but most of further Asia has India to thank for its most widely spread religion—Buddhism. The West today—with increasing respect, thoughtfulness, and admiration—is turning more and more to an examination and an appraisal of India's religious and philosophical institutions.

Moreover, it is interesting to note that of all the far-flung tribe of Indo-European speaking peoples—the Slavs, Germans, Romans, Greeks, and the rest—only the Indians have evolved and clung to internally developed religion. India has contributed to the world two major religions, Hinduism and Buddhism, and a third equally significant religion, Jainism, which is restricted to the Indian subcontinent. Some twenty centuries ago the West gave up its own indigenous religious systems in favor of Christianity, which came out of the Middle East and out of Judaism; Persia adopted Islam some thirteen centuries ago. In the West and in Iran the religious record is one of revolution: a casting off of the old (though not as thoroughly as some would have it) and an embracing of the new. In India the record is one of evolution, of an organic growth, and of continuity.

Thus it is that the religion and philosophy of traditional India receive the most attention in this volume. I should like to make my reasons for this emphasis clear.

It is becoming more and more fashionable in the West to turn to Hindu and Buddhist religion and philosophy not for enrichment primarily, but for solace, enlightenment, or for some other reason. This is essentially a seeking of solutions in the East for the trials and dilemmas of the West. Where the quest is genuine, it is commendable and should be encouraged; but the selections in this volume are not offered with any such cross-cultural synthesis in view. Rather, these selections are offered partly because they throw a modicum of light on subjects that are worthwhile in themselves and because they represent Indian achievements of interest and import—achievements that are more than purely Indian, that are universally human, and that reflect something of ourselves.

Perhaps the most compelling reason for the emphasis on the area of religion and philosophy is the conviction that no culture can be understood without some appreciation of its religious and philosophical foundations—its ethical base. To try to achieve some understanding of India without an acquaintance with this base is like trying to come to grips with Renaissance Italy or modern Switzerland outside the context of Greek thought, Roman law, and Christian theology. It is in its religious and philosophical institutions that the prime key to an understanding of any people is to be found. We know next to nothing of a people if we never come to know something of the elements that guide and impel them and mold them; if we know nothing of their own view of life and their place in it, of their aspirations and hopes for this life, and perhaps for some other life.

This volume is in three main sections. The first is a kind of stage setting—selections on the land itself, its physical features and their importance, the people, and the prehistory of the subcontinent. The following section is that dealing with the religion and philosophy of traditional India. This is followed by a few selections on specific achievements of traditional Indian culture and on its secular facets.

Much has of necessity been omitted or slighted. There is nothing here dealing, for instance, with the art of India, with achievements in the sciences, and with caste. My excuse is that limitations of space have necessitated passing over many worthwhile topics. Some topics, such as art, do not lend themselves readily to brief treatment; furthermore, to be effective, a treatment of the art of India should be accompanied by visual materials. Another glaring omission, caste, is an inordinately complex subject, still the subject of much heated debate as to its origins and even as to its exact nature and working. Caste is alluded to in several of the selections, and I have decided to leave it at that.

This is probably the only "source book" that doesn't consist of primary source material—that is, the records and documents themselves that treat of the matter under discussion. My reasons for restricting myself to other than primary sources are quite simple. The most obvious reason is, of course, that the primary sources on any single topic in this volume are vast enough to absorb the energies and efforts of a lifetime; selection of one item from such an assortment of riches becomes almost impossible. But the most compelling reason is that I am thoroughly convinced that ten passages from, say, the Bhagavad Gītā—no matter how well chosen—cannot come close to giving as clear a picture of the import and the essence of that work as the three selections by Professor Franklin Edgerton here included. Furthermore, there is the need to translate the sources of our knowledge of traditional India and this, in my view, effectively robs a document of its character and value as a true primary source. Primary sources are for the specialist; and we can benefit more from his insights into what, after all, is an integrated whole than by reading short, out-of-context bits and pieces.

I have therefore largely bypassed primary sources in the firm belief that synthesis, often the life work of scholar-specialists with a thorough command of the subject, can better serve as an introduction to a difficult subject. Should the present selections impel the reader to further inquiry in greater scope and depth—and one naturally hopes that it will—its purpose as a modest introduction will have been more than served.

The approach to the subject of traditional India has been, of necessity, highly selective; and because it is selective, it is also subjective. Another Indologist or missionary, anthropologist, or linguist would probably offer entirely different selections as valid and revealing as these. In my view the readings in the present volume represent succinct, serious, revealing, and highly readable treatments of certain aspects of traditional Indian culture. Moreover, they represent readings that I have myself enjoyed, and from which I think I may have also profited.

Finally, no book is a one-man effort, and this is by no means the exception. Gratitude must be expressed in several quarters. To the original publishers of the selections presented here, to whom due acknowledgement is made; to the admirable Mrs. Sharon Kline of the Center for Southern Asian Studies, The University of Michigan, for much of the typing and for that invaluable attention to details that invariably escaped me; to my student, Miss Helen Ullrich, for assistance in making the selections; and to my wife, Frances, for proofreading, hand-holding, and for the simple and wonderful fact of being my wife.

## A NOTE ON TRANSLITERATION

*Vowels*

*a, i, u* have roughly the value of the vowels in the English words *putt, pit, put,* respectively.

*ā, ī, ū* have roughly the value of the vowels in the English words *pot, peat, pooch,* respectively.

*ṛ* is a vocalic consonant or semivowel. It may be rendered as the initial consonant and vowel of the English word *rip.*

The series of consonants with a subscript dot—that is, *ṭ, ṭh, ḍ, ḍh, ṇ,* and *ṣ* (but not *ṛ*—see above) are called retroflex consonants; they are produced by placing the tip of the tongue against the roof of the mouth. *ṣ* sounds somewhat like the *sh* in the English words *shoe, ship,* and so on, as does the letter *ś*; and they may be so rendered.

*ṃ* may be pronounced in the same position as the following consonant. That is, before *t* it is pronounced like *n,* before *b* like *m,* and so on.

The letters followed by *h*: *bh, dh, th,* and so on, are called aspirates. They are pronounced much like the simple *b, d, t,* and so on, of English, but are followed by a strong puff of air.

The rest of the sounds in the transliterated material may be produced much as their English equivalents.

# 1

# THE LAND OF INDIA

## A. L. Basham

This first selection requires little comment; it treats of the land and serves to set the scene on which the story of Indian civilization is played. It serves, moreover, to bring out in quite poetic form the importance of natural phenomena in the lives of the people of India. No one who has ever witnessed the onset of the rains along the Western Ghats remains unawed before its overwhelming immensity; nor can one fail to react joyfully to the almost overnight transition from dull brown to tender green that follows. On the other hand, a sparse or late (often both) monsoon frequently means disaster. India is a land in which nature is indeed both bounteous and cruel; and particularly her meteorological waywardness can be a severe source of trial to a people whose overwhelming majority depends so desperately and directly upon her. Still, I would stress the point made by Basham in this selection that to speculate on the effects of nature's waywardness on the character of the Indian peoples is chancy at best. It is, however, a point that has proved an attractive one on which to speculate, and doubtless it will continue to do so.

The ancient civilization of India grew up in a sharply demarcated subcontinent bounded on the north by the world's largest mountain range—the chain of the Himālayas, which, with its extensions to east and west, divides India from the rest of Asia and the world. The barrier, however, was at no time an insuperable one, and at all periods both settlers and traders have found their way over the high and desolate passes into India, while Indians have carried their commerce and culture beyond her frontiers by the same route. India's isolation has never been complete, and the effect of the mountain wall in developing her unique civilization has often been overrated.

The importance of the mountains to India is not so much in the isolation which they give her, as in the fact that they are the source of her two great rivers. The clouds drifting northwards and westwards in the rainy season discharge the last of their moisture on the high peaks, whence, fed by ever-melting snow, innumerable streams flow southward, to meet in the great river systems of the Indus and the Ganges. On their way they pass through small and fertile plateaux, such as the valleys of Kashmīr and Nepāl, to debouch on the great plain.

Of the two river systems, that of the Indus, now mainly in Pākistān, had the earliest civilization, and gave its name to India.[1] The Fertile Plain of the Panjāb ("Five Rivers"), watered by the five great tributaries of the Indus—the Jhelam, Chenāb, Rāvī, Beās and Satlaj—had a high culture over two thousand years before Christ, which spread down the lower course of the Indus as far as the sea. The lower Indus, in the Pākistān province of Sind, now passes through barren desert, though this was once a well-watered and fertile land.

The basin of the Indus is divided from that of the Ganges by the Thar, or desert of Rājasthān, and by low hills. The watershed, to the northwest of Delhī, has been the scene of many bitter battles since at least 1000 B.C. The western half of the Ganges plain, from the region around Delhī to Patnā, and including the *Doāb,* or the land between the Ganges and its great tributary river Jamnā, has always been the heart of India. Here, in the region once known as *Āryāvarta,* the land of the Āryans, her classical culture was formed. Though generations of unscientific farming, deforestation, and other factors have now much reduced its fertility, it was once among the most productive lands in the world, and has supported a very large population ever since it was brought under the plough. At its mouth in Bengal the Ganges forms a large delta, which even in historical times has gained appreciably on the sea; here it joins the river

[1] The Indians knew this river as *Sindhu,* and the Persians, who found difficulty in pronouncing an initial *s,* called it *Hindu.* From Persia the word passed into Greece, where the whole of India became known by the name of the western river. The ancient Indians knew their subcontinent as *Jambudvīpa* (the continent of the *jambu* tree) or *Bhāratavarṣa* (the Land of the Sons of Bharata, a legendary emperor). The latter name has been in part revived by the present Indian government. With the Muslim invasion the Persian name returned in the form Hindustān, and those of its inhabitants who followed the old religion became known as Hindūs.

Brahmaputra, which flows from Tibet by way of the Valley of Assam, the easternmost outpost of Hindu culture.

South of the great plain is a highland zone, rising to the chain of the Vindhya mountains. These are by no means as impressive as the Himālayas, but have tended to form a barrier between the North, formerly called Hindustān, and the Peninsula, often known as the Deccan (meaning simply "south"), a term used sometimes for the whole peninsula, but more often for its northern and central portions. Most of the Deccan is a dry and hilly plateau, bordered on either side by long ranges of hills, the Western and Eastern Ghāts. Of these two ranges the western is the higher, and therefore most of the rivers of the Deccan, such as the Mahānadī, the Godāvarī, the Kistnā or Kṛṣṇā, and the Kāverī, flow eastwards to the sea. Two large rivers only, the Narmadā and the Tāptī, flow westwards. Near their mouths the Deccan rivers pass through plains which are smaller than those of the Ganges but almost as populous. The southeastern part of the Peninsula forms a large plain, the Tamil country, the culture of which was once independent, and is not yet completely unified with that of the North. The Dravidian people of Southern India still speak languages in no way akin to those of the North, and are of a different ethnic character, though there has been much intermixture between Northern and Southern types. Geographically, Ceylon is a continuation of India, the plain of the North resembling that of South India, and the mountains in the centre of the island the Western Ghāts.

From Kashmīr in the North to Cape Comorin in the South the subcontinent is about 2,000 miles long, and therefore its climate varies considerably. The Himālayan region has cold winters, with occasional frost and snow. In the northern plains the winter is cool, with wide variation of day and night temperature, whereas the hot season is almost intolerable. The temperature of the Deccan varies less with the season, though in the higher parts of the plateau nights are cool in winter. The Tamil Plain is continuously hot, but its temperature never rises to that of the northern plains in summer.

The most important feature of the Indian climate is the monsoon, or "the rains." Except along the west coast and in parts of Ceylon rain rarely falls from October to May, when cultivation can only be carried on by carefully husbanding the water of rivers and streams, and raising a winter crop by irrigation. By the end of April growth has practically ceased. The temperature of the plains rises as high as 110° F. or over, and an intensely hot wind blows. Trees shed their leaves, grass is almost completely parched, wild animals often die in large numbers for want of water. Work is reduced to a minimum, and the world seems asleep.

Then clouds appear, high in the sky; in a few days they grow more numerous and darker, rolling up in banks from the sea. At last, in June, the rains come in great downpouring torrents, with much thunder and lightning. The temperature quickly drops, and within a few days the world is green and smiling again. Beasts, birds, and insects reappear, the trees put on new leaves, and the earth is covered with fresh grass. The torrential rains, which fall at intervals for a couple of months and then gradually die away, make travel and all outdoor activity difficult, and often bring epidemics in their wake; but despite these hardships, to the Indian mind the coming of the monsoon corresponds to the coming of spring in Europe. For this reason thunder and lightning, in Europe generally looked on as inauspicious, have no terrors for the Indian, but are welcome signs of the goodness of heaven.

It has often been said that the scale of natural phenomena in India, and her total dependence on the monsoon, have helped to form the character of her peoples. Even today major disasters—such as flood, famine, and plague—are hard to check, and in older times their control was almost impossible. Many other ancient civilizations—such as those of the Greeks, Romans, and Chinese—had to contend with hard winters, which encouraged sturdiness and resource. India, on the other hand, was blessed by a bounteous Nature, who demanded little of man in return for sustenance, but in her terrible anger could not be appeased by any human effort. Hence, it has been suggested, the Indian character has tended to fatalism and quietism, accepting fortune and misfortune alike without complaint.

How far this judgment is a fair one is very dubious. Though an element of quietism certainly existed in the ancient Indian attitude to life, as it does in India today, it was never approved by moralists. The great achievements of ancient India and Ceylon—their immense irrigation works and splendid temples, and the long campaigns of their armies—do not suggest a devitalized people. If the climate had any effect on the Indian character, it was, we believe, to develop a love of ease and comfort, an addiction to the simple pleasures and luxuries so freely given by Nature—a tendency to which the impulse to self-denial and asceticism on the one hand, and occasional strenuous effort on the other, were natural reactions.

# 2

# GEOGRAPHY AND PREHISTORY

## H. G. Rawlinson

In addition to geographical variety, which has been touched upon in the preceding selection, India exhibits almost luxuriant variety in a number of other ways. Her languages today are numerous, springing from four distinct genetic strains: the Indo-European and Dravidian, and the more restricted Mundaric and Tibeto-Burman. Modes of dress, social habits, marriage customs and rites, forms of worship, and the objects of worship themselves—all within the scope of Hinduism but with a bewildering variety of names and epithets—present an almost kaleidoscopic array. Even the lowly cow or buffalo dung cake (which, dried in the sun, is a prime source of domestic heat) shows throughout India considerable variety in shape as well as in the manner in which it is set out to dry.

About 1500 B.C. groups of pastoral nomads, relatively uncivilized, began descending into the plains that we know today as the Punjab—the Land of Five Rivers—doubtless through the mountain passes which seal off the northwestern part of the subcontinent, and of which the most renowned is the Khyber. These people styled themselves Aryan or nobles, and they spoke an Indo-European language, Sanskrit, whose earliest form is called Vedic after the literary monuments, the Vedas, which have preserved it for us. The Aryans apparently liked what they saw in this Land of Five Rivers, for they seem to have settled in rather quickly. These people whom most of us tend to think as *the* Indians were in reality latecomers to the subcontinent; yet their arrival is of the greatest significance, for it marks the beginning of Indian civilization as we know it. To be sure, the Aryan institutions, particularly their religious institutions, underwent an almost radical change—certainly within the first thou-

From H. G. Rawlinson, C.I.E., *India, A Short Cultural History* (rev. ed., 1954). Reprinted by permission of Frederick A. Praeger, Inc.

sand years of their arrival. Still the change was an organic and Indian one, and the Aryans wrote the first chapter in a story that is still ongoing at the present time

Above, I used the term "uncivilized" in referring to the first Aryan migrants and I did so deliberately, though perhaps in a more literal sense than is customary. The Aryans were not city dwellers but nomads; not long after their arrival in the subcontinent, they did begin to settle in cities—that is, to become "civilized"—but their urban settlements were never for some reason quite up to the standards of those of their predecessors in the region. The Aryans did not blunder into a wilderness, but into an area which had once known—possibly still knew at their arrival—a highly sophisticated urban culture going back beyond the middle of the third millennium B.C. Whether the Aryans could not learn or chose not to learn civilized manners from the people of the Indus Valley Civilization, we shall probably never know for certain. (The Indus Civilization could have already disappeared, or the Aryans could have destroyed it.) The fact remains that the early urban centers of the Aryans were decidedly inferior to the magnificence of Mohenjo-daro and Harappa, and seem to owe little if anything to those two centers of Indus Civilization.

The disappearance of the Indus Civilization is a case of circumstantial evidence of epic proportions. We have, on the one hand, the rather abrupt disappearance of what archeological evidence tells us was a flourishing culture, and without definite signs of serious deterioration; on the other hand, we have the arrival of a not overly refined group of pastoral nomads coinciding with that disappearance or decline. There the case, for all but the partisan, must rest; for though the evidence is there, it remains strictly circumstantial, and we have as yet no way of linking the arrival of the Aryans directly to the disappearance of the Indus Civilization. A number of scholars have pointed the finger of accusation at the Aryans, as the two following selections indicate, but the guilt of those immigrants is far from establised beyond reasonable doubt.

We do not know for certain who the authors of this remarkable civilization were; it is another of those mysteries that make the scholar's life at once interesting and somewhat frustrating. The story of the Indus Civilization belongs to the field of archeology, for its people left us no other record; or rather, they left us what we take to be a record of some kind in the pictographic symbols on their seals, but it is one which, unfortunately, we cannot read. Conjecture as to who the inhabitants of the Indus Civilization were, whether indigenous or themselves intruders, has not been found wanting; but again the record is silent. It is nevertheless a remarkable record, as the two following selections indicate, and one must agree with

Rawlinson that the discovery of the Indus Civilization is "one of the most important discoveries of modern archeology."

A note of caution: The Hyderabad mentioned here is a city in Sind in present-day Pakistan; it is not to be confused with the former princely state of Hyderabad—the domain of the famous Nizam—and its capital of the same name, which is today the capital of the modern Indian state of Andhra Pradesh. The latter two Hyderabads are in the Deccan, in central India.

The subcontinent known to Western nations by the name of India is, roughly speaking, a gigantic rhomboid, with an area of about 1,575,000 square miles and a population of over 400 millions. This country is peopled by a large number of ethnic groups in every stage of development, from the aboriginal inhabitants of the central forests to the highly cultured men of letters of its universities, speaking a bewildering number of languages, and differing widely in physical appearance and social customs. It would be inaccurate to apply the term "nation" to ancient India. "The people of Intu," says the Chinese traveller Hiuen Tsang, "call their country by different names, according to the district." Āryāvarta in Sanskrit and Hindustan or Hind in later dialects refer to the Gangetic plain; India was a term originally borrowed by the Greeks from the Persians, who applied it exclusively to the country watered by the Sindhu or Indus river, the inhabitants of which were known as Indians or Hindus. From time to time an Indian Napoleon arose who would temporarily knit this vast congeries of peoples into a coherent whole, and the Mogul Emperors even imposed a single official language, Persian. But it was reserved for her latest conquerors to introduce, not only a common tongue, but common political aspirations, the growth of which had been immensely facilitated by the opening up of communications, the spread of education, and the diffusion of Western political ideas. This lack of national consciousness is perhaps the main reason why pre-Muhammadan India had no historians. Her vast literature contains no Herodotus or Thucydides, no Tacitus or Livy; the very memory of her greatest ruler, the Emperor Asoka, was forgotten, until European scholars at the beginning of the nineteenth century laboriously reconstructed the story by piecing together the fragments which had survived the ravages of time.

And yet through all this apparent diversity there runs an underlying unity. The conception of a national religion, it has been said, is the only germ to be found in ancient times of the idea of Indian nationality. In spite of all differences of language, race, and sect, from the Himālayas to Cape Comorin the fundamental principles of the Hindu religion hold their immemorial sway over the vast majority of the population. These may be summed up as the almost universal belief in the authority of the Vedas and the sacredness of the cow, the worship of the great gods Siva and Vishnu in their innumerable aspects, and the institution of caste. Caste, perhaps, more than any other feature, distinguishes India from the rest of the world. Its vitality is immense. It has survived the attacks of religious reformers from within and hostile influences from without, and even today shows few signs of decay. Now, however, a fresh factor has appeared in the wave of nationalism which has swept over the subcontinent and has integrated the whole country into the two independent states of India (Bhārat) and Pākistān. Whether caste will be able to survive the disintegrating impact of this new onslaught of western influences remains to be seen.[1]

The history of India is to a great extent determined by geographical conditions. To the north, she is shut off by the gigantic mountain wall of the Himālayas, running along her northern frontier from Afghanistan to Assam for 1,600 miles, and forming an almost impenetrable obstacle to intercourse with the rest of Asia except from the northwest. Here the barrier is pierced where it turns southward by openings through which the Indus and Kābul rivers flow into India. At the northwest angle is the Khyber Pass, 3,400 feet above sea level, with the city of Peshāwar, the ancient Pushpapura, at its mouth. South of this are the Kurram, Tochi, and Gumal Passes, and the famous Bolān Pass. Between the Bolān Pass and the sea, the Sind-Baluchistan boundary is formed by the Hālā, Brāhui and Pab mountains; but these are much less formidable than the northern ranges, and there is a gap between their southern extremity and the coast. Through the Khyber runs the road to Kābul. Kābul, again, is the focus of a number of routes, running northwards to Balkh and Central Asia, and westwards to Herāt, Meshed, and Asia Minor, while through the Bolān the road reaches Kandahār, another great meeting place of ancient routes to Seistan and Persia. All these approaches to India have played a decisive part in her history. By them, from immemorial times, migrating tribes, peaceful traders, and conquering armies have poured over the Iranian plateau into the fertile plains lying beyond the mountains.

India falls into four main cultural divisions, each dominated by

[1] Percival Spear, *India, Pakistan and the West* (1949), Chap. XIII.

its river systems. These are the basins of the Indus and of the Ganges, the Deccan plateau, and southern or peninsular India. Rivers play an all-important part in Indian history, both as a means of communication and a source of water supply; hence it is not surprising that so many of her earliest inhabitants settled along the banks of the great streams. The westernmost of these divisions is the alluvial plain watered by the Indus and its four tributaries: the Sutlej, the Rāvi, the Chenab, and the Jhelum, and hence known as the Punjab, or Land of Five Rivers. South of the confluence of these streams lies Sind, the land of the river Sindhu, the Vedic name for the Indus. A fact of which the historian must not lose sight is the changes which have occurred in the course of time in the beds of the Indian rivers. Flowing as they do through soft, sandy banks, they have altered their channels many times in the course of history. The Sutlej, united with the Saraswatī and Ghaggar, used to form a huge stream —the Hakrā—which flowed through what is now desert land in Bahawālpur. The Hakrā only dried up in the eighteenth century. The modern Indus delta is of recent origin. At one time the river flowed into the Rann of Cutch.

The Indus and Ganges basins are separated by the Thar, or Rājputāna desert, and are linked by a narrow corridor running between it and the Himālayas, which roughly follows the course of the Jumna river. This corridor, the ancient Kurukshetra, has been happily named the cockpit of India, for here, owing to its strategic importance, the fate of the country has been decided on innumerable occasions. The Gangetic plain, watered by the Ganges and her great tributaries—the Jumna, the Chambal, the Gumtī, the Gogra, and the Son—with innumerable smaller streams, is an immense, fertile tract, with an area of 300,000 square miles and a breadth of 90 to 300 miles. Its vast natural resources and its great waterways have made it the scene of the most striking events in India's history. Along the banks of the Ganges many of the great Hindu empires of the past, with their splendid cities, sprang up and flourished. "Mother Ganges" is, above all, the sacred river of India. Hardwār, where, rising from an icy Himalayan cave she debouches into the plain, and Prayāga (Allahābād) where she joins her "twin" the Yamunā or Jumna, are places of pilgrimage visited by millions of pious Hindus. Not less holy is the venerable city of Kāsī or Benares, upon her lower banks. Near her mouth she is joined by another mighty river, the Brahmaputra or "Son of Brahma," which flows through gigantic gorges, from the mountains of Tibet, to pass through Assam and Eastern Bengal.

The southern boundary of the Gangetic plain is formed by the Vindhya mountains and their offshoots. These are sandstone ranges, rising to about 3,000 feet, and formerly clad with dense and impenetrable jungle, the Dandaranyaka or Mahākāntāra of Vedic and Epic days, beyond which the Aryan-speaking tribes found it difficult to penetrate. These ranges form the northern edge of the Deccan plateau. The Deccan, or South Land, is the most ancient part of India, and was once probably linked up with an Austral continent stretching far to the eastward. On the western side, the plateau terminates with the Western Ghauts or "stairs," a steep mountain wall running roughly parallel with the shores of the Arabian Sea for about 600 miles. This has weathered into a number of flat-topped peaks, easily convertible into almost impregnable fortresses, which were destined to play an important part in the history of the Marāthā nation. The Ghauts shut off the Deccan from the sea, and are pierced by occasional passes, which could only be surmounted in former days by pack animals. Farther south, however, is the all-important Pālghāt, or Gap of Coimbatore, about 20 miles broad, which leads from the Malabar Coast to the plains of the Carnatic. On the eastern side, the Ghauts are much less steep and continuous, and the two ranges terminate in the lofty peaks of the Nīlgiri or Blue Mountains. The rivers of the Indian peninsula, with the exception of the Tāptī and the Narbadā, flow into the Bay of Bengal. The principal streams are the Mahānadī, the Godāverī and the Krishnā, with their tributaries. The Tungabadhrā, the chief tributary of the Kistna, is usually looked upon as the southern boundary of the Deccan. Beyond lies the Tamil country; in the center are the Cardamon Hills, but for the most part it consists of broad plains, watered by the Pennār and Kāverī rivers. Physical features have tended to isolate southern India from the rest of the country, and it early developed a culture essentially its own.

Climatic conditions have played a large part in Indian history. The martial races have been chiefly bred in the dry, hilly districts of the northwest and center and the deserts of Rājputāna, where a livelihood can only be wrested from the soil by intense effort, and, even then, has to be supplemented by raids upon more favored neighbours; the fertile, low-lying plains of Bengal, on the other hand, have been inhabited by peaceful, unwarlike cultivators. The destinies of a large part of the peninsula depend to a considerable extent upon the seasonal rainfall brought by the monsoons, currents of moisture-laden air which sweep across the country from the Arabian Sea from June to October. The heaviest precipitation occurs upon the Western Ghauts, where the rainclouds first strike upon the Indian coast, the southern slopes of the Himālayas north of Bengal, and the Assam Hills. Here the rainfall amounts to over 100 inches in the year; in the Deccan and the Delhi district it amounts to nearly 25 inches, or about the same as London. In Sind and the Rājputāna desert, it is only five inches at the present day. But it must be borne in mind that a series of climatic changes have taken place in Central Asia, including northwestern India, which have materially affected the course of history, as they brought about the migration of peoples from the desiccated areas in search of new pastures. Formerly, India was by no means as isolated as she is at present. In what are now the arid wastes of Baluchistan may be seen abundant traces of former cultivation; and Khotan, now a rainless desert, was the seat of a flourishing civilization as late as the ninth century A.D. Sind, now arid except where it is irrigated, was once densely populated, with an equable climate and a fertile soil. The Indus valley seals exhibit rhinoceroses, elephants, and tigers, all inhabitants of well-watered jungles, and unknown in Sind today. The Arab historians speak of Sind as an oasis surrounded by deserts, and as late as the fourteenth century, Timūr lost his horses at Multan owing to heavy rains. Strabo[2] speaks of the violent monsoon rain of the spring and early summer of 326 B.C. in the Taxila district, which hampered Alexander's operations. Man, by clearing forests, damming rivers, and erecting irrigation works, has played his part in bringing about these changes.[3]

Peninsular India is more dependent on the monsoon than the plains of the north, where the Indus and the Ganges and most of their tributaries are fed by the periodic melting of the Himalayan snows. The rivers of the center and south have no such advantages, and dry up when the monsoon rains fail. This formerly led to periodic famines, in which the death rate was often appalling. These catastrophes are now minimized by irrigation works and by the opening up of communications, which enables the ready transfer of

[2] Strabo, *Geography*, Vol. XV, pp. 690 ff.

[3] Deforestation and malaria are two factors which have played an important part in Indian history. See F. J. Richards, "Geographical Factors in Indian Archaeology," *Indian Antiquary*, Vol. LXII (1933), pp. 235 ff.

supplies to the affected district. During the rainy season, in days when metaled roads were unknown and rivers unbridged, there was a general cessation from activities. Wandering bands of monks retired to their monasteries and armies went into winter quarters until the Dasara festival in mid-October ushered in the commencement of the campaigning season.

There is evidence that parts of India have been inhabited by human races from a remote time. Palaeolithic and neolithic remains have been discovered as far apart as Bellary in Madras and Mirzāpur in the United Provinces. In the former district a neolithic potter's workshop has been brought to light. Near Tinnivelly, prehistoric cemeteries covering large areas have been unearthed, and there is abundant evidence of ancient pearl and conch-shell fisheries at the mouth of the Tamraparni river, and of gold-workings, probably of neolithic origin, at Maski in the Nizam's Dominions. At Mirzāpur and other places, megalithic cemeteries, apparently of the iron age, have been discovered. Crude drawings in red pigment are found on cave walls in the Bellary and Wynaad districts and other localities. From the evidence, it appears that neolithic man in southern India reached a fairly advanced degree of civilization. He knew the use of the potter's wheel, and how to cut and hollow out timber and dress skins. He made ornaments of conch-shell, pearls, and gold beads. He cultivated crops in jungle clearings, and had domesticated the dog, ox, and goat. In southern India, stone tools were replaced by iron; in the north, copper was employed, and the absence of a bronze age is conspicuous. Finds of copper implements have been made from time to time. At Gungeria in the Central Provinces, a hoard of over 400 objects was discovered, including shouldered axes, harpoons, barbed spears and swords, and silver laminae.[4]

We now come to what may be described as one of the most important discoveries of modern archaeology.[5] Mysterious seals, bearing pictographic signs in an unknown script, had been discovered at Harappā in the Montgomery District of the Punjab many years ago, but it was not until 1922 that Mr. R. D. Banerji, while working on a second-century Buddhist stupa at Mohenjo-daro, 25 miles south of Lārkhāna in Sind, came across the remains of a great prehistoric city belonging to the chalcolithic age. This was excavated under the auspices of Sir John Marshall, the Director-General of Archaeology,

[4] *Cambridge History of India,* Vol. I, pp. 612-15.

[5] See Sir J. Marshall, *Mohenjo-daro and the Indus Civilization* (1931); L. E. Mackay, *The Indus Civilization* (1935).

with surprising results. The town is well laid out. Its streets are at right angles, running due north and south and east and west. The main street, which is 33 feet wide, has been traced for over half a mile and is unpaved. The side roads are about half this width. The buildings are of burnt brick set in mud mortar. No stone is used and the absence of any kind of ornamentation is conspicuous. The windows and doors open upon the main street, and it was probable that some were several stories high, with flat roofs. An unusual feature of the houses is the presence of bathrooms, and also of an elaborate drainage system, greatly in advance of anything known in later India. For this purpose, pottery drain pipes and receptacles were laid down, communicating with the street drain or gutter. No temple has been discovered, but a large public bath, 39 feet by 23, has been unearthed. This bath, which was rendered watertight, is provided with steps leading down to the water, a promenade, and compartments for the bathers. Ingenious arrangements for filling and emptying it are provided. Just to the south of the bathroom is a large building, over 200 feet long and 100 feet wide, which may have been the royal palace.

The inhabitants were highly artistic, and the numerous objects found in the course of excavation throw a flood of light upon their social customs and habits. The most numerous are the remarkable steatite seals or amulets, of which large numbers have been collected. Their precise use is unknown, but the fact that they are perforated at the back suggests that they were worn round the neck on a string. They are beautifully carved and glazed; the commonest objects represented on them are a magnificent Brahminy bull, and a "unicorn" (perhaps the urus ox seen in profile), which appears to be eating out of a manger. Tigers, elephants, rhinoceroses, short-horned bulls, antelopes, buffaloes, and the gharial or fish-eating crocodile also figure on the seals, but the absence of the cow and horse are significant. Many of the seals bear brief inscriptions in a pictographic script which still remains undeciphered. It is probable that they give the names of the owners. Besides the seals, a number of figures in steatite, clay and limestone have been discovered. One of these shows a man with narrow eyes, thick lips and flat nose, a short abundant beard, and a clean-shaven lip. His hair is confined by a fillet, and he wears a shawl or robe ornamented with a trefoil pattern similar to that found on some of the pottery. Small figurines of burnt clay—including some charming children's toys in the shape of various birds and beasts, a toy cart, and an animal which moves its head—

have been discovered in great numbers. The pottery is fine and varied. It was turned on the fast lathe, and a variety of beautifully shaped specimens have been found, including large storage jars, flat basins with a high foot, and cylindrical and pointed bases. Spouts and handles are very rare. The pottery is usually coated with a slip of red ochre, often so highly burnished that it has the appearance of Chinese lacquer. Very often it is ornamented with a pattern of concentric circles in black, and occasionally with figures of trees, birds, and animals. Some of the pottery is ornamented with clay knobs: this knobbed ware is unique in India. Faïence was used for bracelets, statuettes, and beads.

The Indus valley folk were skilled metalworkers. They employed gold, silver, lead, and copper, and knew how to make bronze. The finest specimen of their bronze work is an adze, about ten inches long, with a socket for a handle. Beakers were made of copper, silver, or lead; these were either beaten or cast. Saws, chisels, knives, razors, and other metal implements have been discovered, but the weapons (copper spearheads, arrowheads, and swords) are of an inferior quality, and suggest that the users were unwarlike in their habits. The *cire perdue* process of casting was practised, and an exquisite little bronze figure of a dancing girl is an almost perfect piece of work. Jewelry, in the shape of bangles and necklaces, was commonly worn, and the latter consisted of beads of jadeite, lapis-lazuli, amazonite, and gold. Weights and scales suggest an advanced state of civilization. Among amusements, dancing to the accompaniment of the drum, marbles, and some kind of game played with a marker board and pieces appear to have been practised.

Much light is thrown by the discoveries upon the religion of the Indus valley. The most common object of worship appears to have been the Mother Goddess, whose cult was spread all over Asia Minor. She is represented in numerous pottery figurines, and on seals and amulets. Another goddess appears as horned, and in association with a sacred pipal tree. A horned three-faced god, who is represented upon one of the seals in a seated attitude, surrounded by animals, has been identified with the Indian Siva-Mahādeva, and this hypothesis is strengthened by the discovery of representations of the Lingam, the symbol of Siva. Whether the animals represented on the seals were objects of worship is unknown, but conspicuous among them is the bull, the Nandi of later times, and Siva's vāhan or vehicle.

Various burial rites seem to have been in use, perhaps by different stocks or tribes. At Mohenjo-daro, the absence of a cemetery seems to point to cremation, but a large burial ground has been found at Harappā. The ashes were sometimes placed in urns; at other times unburnt bones were collected and buried in jars.

The Indus valley culture was widely distributed. Harappā and Mohenjo-daro are 400 miles apart, and numerous sites have been located all along the Indus, as far as Hyderabad, more than 100 miles to the south; in Baluchistān and the Makrān, 150 miles to the west, and as far north as Rupar on the Sutlej at the foot of the Simla hills. Examination of the skeletal remains show that the people were of a mixed race, the Mediterranean being the preponderating type. The skulls agree with those found at Al Ubaid and Kish, and belong to a dolichocephalic people. This—together with some general resemblances between pottery, beads, tools, and weapons—suggests that the Indus valley folk were an intrusive stock, who shared a common ancestry with the Sumerians; no doubt they found a more primitive race already in possession of the country when they entered it, and, as usually happens, intermarried with the earlier inhabitants, and to some extent absorbed their customs. Recent discoveries of pottery seem to show that they came by way of the Mula Pass and the coastal road which runs through Las Bela and the Makrān and crosses the Hab near Karachi.[6] But they were no mere immigrants: they developed a type of civilization which was characteristically Indian. The date of Mohenjo-daro is approximately settled by the discovery of what is undoubtedly an Indus valley seal at Tel-Asmar, in a stratum which may be dated circa 2500 B.C. Other finds of Mesopotamian origin in Sind and *vice versa* confirm this. Allowing for the building of the successive cities at Mohenjo-daro, we may perhaps date their arrival at about 1000 years earlier. More we cannot say until a clue is found to the pictographs. This will perhaps be provided by the discovery of a bilingual seal; we shall then be able to decide whether the language spoken in the Indus valley was of Sumerian origin or not.

What caused the downfall of the Indus valley culture? A variety of explanations have been offered—desiccation, an alteration in the bed of the Indus, epidemic disease, or invasion. We infer from the evidence that the inhabitants were a peaceful folk, whose great wealth must have offered a tempting prey to the wild tribes from the hills, and there are reasons for thinking that Mohenjo-daro was sacked and the inhabitants put to the sword. Groups of skeletons, including women and children, have been found, some in a large room,

[6] *Memoirs, Archaeological Survey of India,* No. 48, pp. 153 ff.

others at the foot of a staircase leading down to a well, and others again in a street. Their contorted attitudes suggest that they met a violent death. It seems probable that the invaders who sacked Mohenjo-daro and Harappā were the Indo-Aryans, and that the Indus valley folk were the Dāsas or Dasyu of the Rig Veda. There is evidence that this took place about 1500 B.C., when the Indus civilization was on the wane.

## NOTE ON THE INDUS VALLEY CULTURE

Since the above was written, extensive researches by Professor Stuart Piggot (*Prehistoric Indian,* 1952) and Sir Mortimer Wheeler (*The Indus Civilization,* 1953) have revealed that the Indus valley culture extended from Rupar at the foot of the Simla hills to the Arabian Sea 300 miles west of Karachi, with twin capitals at Harappā and Mohenjo-daro. The portrait described on page 18 may be that of a priest-king of the latter capital. After their sack by the Aryan tribesmen, the Indus valley folk—who, according to the Rev. H. Heras, S.J.—were proto-Dravidians, appear to have emigrated to southern India, leaving behind them a linguistic "island" in the modern Brahuis. Father Heras claims that the Indus pictographs are in the Tamil language, and he professes to have found a clue to them.

# 3

# THE INDUS CIVILIZATION

## Sten Konow and Poul Tuxen

While this selection covers some of the material touched upon in the one preceding, it goes a bit farther and brings up for discussion a point that is of much import for the following section: For what, if anything, is Indian civilization indebted to its precursor of the Indus Valley?

Here again we come up against a second case of massive circumstantial evidence. The archeological story of the earlier civilization hints broadly in its iconography at origins for motifs of the later one. But in no case is identification of any single element in Indian civilization with a corresponding one in the Indus Valley so obvious as to be taken as established beyond dispute; there is always the negative evidence of no explicit connection of one civilization with the other to stand in the way of positive identification. The Vedas themselves, the Aryans' earliest and most important documents, are notably reticent on any contact with prior inhabitants of their new land, except for those tantalizing references in the Ṛg Veda to *dāsas* or *dasyus* (slaves), an apparently despised, dark-skinned, and subject people. Again, however, these references offer only circumstantial evidence.

But it is in the realm of thought that speculation is perhaps most tempting and most risky. It cannot be emphasized strongly enough that speculation on the indebtedness of Indian civilization to its precursor places one onto extremely shaky ground. Of course, it is difficult to imagine two peoples apparently living in close proximity for some centuries and eventually intermarrying without some synthesis being produced. It is not unlikely that the Aryans, as Konow puts it, "became Indianized."

It is reasonable to assume that there are non-Aryan elements in the Indian culture that begins to take shape around the seventh pre-Christian century. But what these elements are, and to what extent indigenous systems might have influenced the development of this uniquely Indian culture, we simply cannot say. (We implicitly acknowledge influence when we speak of the culture as "Indian," do we not?) The record is not at all clear. It has been said that some of the salient features of Indian religion and philosophy—such as rebirth, *karma,* and *ahiṃsā* or nonviolence—are non-Aryan, since India does not share these features with her cousins with whom she shares a common linguistic origin, and since it is difficult to see clear origins for them in the early Aryan literature prior to the literature of the Upaniṣads; and the Upaniṣads can be termed the turning point from Brahmanism to Hinduism, from Vedic to genuinely Indian culture. It is further argued that such elements (*karma, saṃsāra,* and the rest) are more apt to be intrusions from indigenous pre-Aryan and therefore non-Aryan systems; and that these systems are taken in to form a genuine synthesis—with its roots in Aryan belief or accommodated to it—as the Aryans settle in their new home, mix with the indigenous peoples, and begin to take them into their community.

While this possibility cannot be denied, neither can it be positively affirmed with any satisfactory degree of certainty; it remains merely a possibility. Since Sten Konow wrote the following selection, much more has been learned about the Indus Civilization. We are, however, no closer to knowing who the people were, nor to answering any of the knotty problems touched upon above. We do not know, and perhaps may never know, what were the religious beliefs of the Indus Civilization. The subject is touched upon again in the selection, "The Origins of Hindu Speculation," by Franklin Edgerton.

In 1922 the Indian scholar Rakhal Das Banerji from Bengal began to excavate a mound in the Larkhana district in Sind, between the Indus and an old branch of this river. It was called Mohenjo Daro, and this name was, wrongly, considered to mean "Dead men's mound." On the top was a Buddhist structure, which seemed to belong to the first centuries A.D., and to begin with there was nothing specially remarkable about the finds.

As he dug downwards, however, they gradually became different. *Inter alia* he found several curious seals of a kind which had long ago been recovered at Harappa in the Panjab, at an old bed of the river Ravi, inscribed with signs which looked like letters. These had been eagerly studied by eminent epigraphists, but without success. It was then a likely assumption that we had come across remnants of an old forgotten civilization, which had once flourished in Sind and in Panjab. Other sites of the same kind have since been found or discovered by photographing from the air, and we now know that we have to do with an extensive territory, which towards the east reaches at least to the Ganges, and in the west through Afghanistan and Balochistan towards the Persian Gulf.

It has been spoken of as the Indus Civilization, because it was the finds in Sind which first opened our eyes to its existence, but most scholars are inclined to think that it formed part of a culture extending over a great part of the whole ancient world, from China in the east perhaps to Egypt in the west.

It has also been thought possible to arrive at an approximate dating. Antiquities which have evidently been transferred from the Indus territory have been found in Mesopotamia in strata from circa 2800 B.C., and the prevailing opinion is now that we may have to go back to about 3000 B.C. or even earlier. And this old civilization was much superior to that of the old Aryan invaders of India, and much older.

In some places we seem to be able to trace a deterioration, and then the old civilization disappears. It has been supposed that this may have been a consequence of the Aryan invasion, and a saying of an eminent German scholar has been quoted in this connection, that the much-admired old songs of the Indo-Aryans are barbarian hymns to barbarian gods.

It has already been indicated above that some curious signs have been found on several seals and antiquities; they are far too numerous to allow us to think of an alphabet, but they might be a kind of hieroglyphs or pictographs. Some scholars thought they could trace similar signs on prehistoric Chinese antiquities and also, even in quite modern times, on Easter Island. It has also been attempted to derive some of the letters of the oldest known Indian alphabet from this source. But it has not been possible to get further than to more or less unlikely guesses.

The discovery of this highly developed pre-Aryan civilization has raised new problems for the student of Indian culture and Indian religions. One of the first inferences we must draw is that Indian applied art, which plays such a great role in the decoration of religious buildings, is largely indebted to it. Among the Aryan Indians this art does not seem to have been the concern of the upper classes. But in the Indus Civilization it was highly developed. One find, a headless statuette, shows an artistic feeling and technique which seems to be inexplicable at such an early time; but Sir John Marshall states that it was found in such circumstances that it cannot have come down subsequently from higher strata. It is made from a fine red stone, which must have been imported from outside, but we cannot say whence. Nothing of the same kind has come to light in the Indo-Hellenic or any other Indian school. The round belly reminds us of the Parkham statue in the Mathura Museum. We seem to be justified to think that much of the best products of Indian sculpture has its roots in the Indus Civilization. Another statuette, found in similar circumstances, is made of dark grey schist and represents a dancer, standing on his right leg, with the body turned to the left and the left leg raised. There seems to have been three heads, and Sir John is probably right in thinking of a prototype of the dancing Śiva, Śiva Natesan. And we also remember Kālidāsa's invocation, Kumārasambhava II, 3, of Brahmā trimūrti, the three-shaped god Brahmā, who was one before creation, but subsequently split himself up for the development of the three *guṇas,* qualities.

Without any doubt we are on religious ground in the case of some primitive images. On a seal we have a god who has been compared with a male figure on the Gundestrup vessel. He sits on his haunches on a throne. On one side of him an elephant and a tiger are standing, on the other a buffalo and a rhinoceros. Below the throne are two deer or harts. The god wears arm-rings and a high cap. We at once think of certain representations of Śiva, Kali's wild consort, but also of images of the Buddha, and we are no doubt justified, in both cases, to assume a continuation of a type from the Indus Civilization.

Then we have several examples of a female deity, with a high headdress and often richly decorated. The breasts are clearly marked, so that the sex is certain. Scholars have, no doubt with right, thought of the Great Mother, who plays such a prominent role in so many religions. She it is, no doubt, also who reappears as Śiva's consort, the deity with the many names, the valiant slayer of demons, but also the beloved mother, whom the Bengalis invoke in their national hymn "Bande Mataram" ("I greet our Mother").

Beautiful they are not, these gods, but bearers of irresistible power, vitality and fertility, death and annihilation. The symbol which we know so well from India, the male and the female member, *linga* and *yoni,* respectively, are frequently met with in the Indus Civilization, as they still are at the present day. The Indo-Aryans had had the same fate as other invaders: They became Indianized.

It is only at a later date that we find more good-looking gods, after the ideal of human beauty had exercised its influence. As the Indians say, "What food man takes, that food his gods take"; that is, man creates his gods in his own image, because it is one and the same eternal reality which underlies man and gods.

And yet, there is a difference: Not so much because the gods have a longer span of life, for they are not individually eternal; their exalted position is at an end when their stock of religious merit is exhausted; but men are, after all, what the Romans called *homines,* "earth-beings," while *deva,* the Sanskrit word for "god," is derived from the root *div,* which denotes "light" and "heaven." They are not limited to one locality, as is often the case with Semitic gods, but they soar through space, and high pillars are raised for them to rest on. And they do not touch the earth when they seem to be walking along. Therefore Damayantī was able to distinguish them from Nala, when they appeared, in his likeness, and presented themselves as suitors.

Just as in modern times, it was not only anthropomorphic deities who were worshipped. In many, often very fine, representations, we see the Indian humped bull (*Bos indicus*). We are reminded of the Brāhmanī bull, which is sacred to Śiva and wanders about as it likes and eats what it wants, as we read in Kipling's *Kim.*

Also common is an apparently one-horned bull standing before something which looks like a censer, and we are irresistibly led to think of some kind of worship. We have representations of elephants, bears, fowls, rhinoceroses, tigers, and so on. It is here also tempting to think of the animal mounts of various gods in Indian religion.

Once we see a horned deity with long hair and arm-rings, standing between two branches of a tree, before which is a half-kneeling woman. We evidently have to do with a tree deity, apparently residing in a Pipal (*Ficus religiosa*), a tree which is viewed with reverence in India. It was under a Pipal that the Buddha had his revelation.

Also water seems to have religious significance. Bathrooms have been found in private houses, and a big bathing establishment has been dug out, which may have been used for sacral lustrations. We remember the ceremonial bathing in sacred wells and rivers in modern India. But nothing has hitherto been found which leads us to think of such—for example, of the holy Ganges—in the Indus Civilization, if we leave out some pictures which seem to represent Nāgas.

On the whole there is so much that reminds us of religious features and conceptions in India at the present day, that the connection cannot be doubted. But we are, of course, mainly reduced to guesses, which can only be considered as provisional.

No structure has been excavated which can, with any certainty, or even probability, be considered to have been a temple, though some of them may also have had their use in worship. In one of them were found several ring stones, which have been supposed to have had something to do with the cult. One big hall with twenty brick-pillars bears some resemblance to Buddhist establishments and basilicas, and reminds us of the problems connected with them, but they may have been intended for ordinary or festival gatherings; and it is worthy of notice that no representations or symbols of *deities* have been found in them.

The old Indo-Aryans had, in the same way, no temples. The gods were worshipped in the open air, or in the house of the worshipper, and real temples have only been found at a later date. And then it is possible to think of foreign, presumably Semitic, influence or, again, of the old Indian saying that man creates his gods in his own image. The kings were called *deva,* "god," and the gods were kings. When the kings got their palaces, the gods would get *theirs*—namely, the temples.

The oldest religious buildings discovered in India are much later than, and have nothing to do with, the Vedic period. They are due to the Buddhists, and none of them is older than the fifth, or the third, century B.C. From excavations at Pataliputra, the capital of the Magadha empire, the present Patna on the Ganges, from the imitation of wooden roofs in ancient cave temples, and other sources, we know that wood was largely used as building material, but wood is perishable. And we have, moreover, no reason for assuming the existence of very old wooden temples in the country.

When the Indians began to build temples, the architectural technique of the Indus Civilization made its influence felt. We can infer this already from the use of bricks in the plinth, for the making of bricks the Indians learnt from the older inhabitants.

About the cult and the racial affinities of the people of the Indus Civilization we know next to nothing. We have already seen what we may infer with regard to their religious conceptions, and as to their possible connection with other ancient peoples. It is tempting to think of the Sumerians, whose name reminds us of the Sauvīras and

and Sindhusauvīras known from fairly old sources as inhabitants of the lower Indus country, but inferences drawn from similarity in designation are usually doubtful.

To the left of what we interpreted as a tree deity, we see a man and a woman. She is raising her hands in adoration, or perhaps rather imploration, while he carries a sickle-shaped knife in his hand. The scene has been interpreted as pointing to human sacrifices; but the interpretation is, of course, uncertain. Such sacrifices are not, however, unknown in later times, as we shall see below in connection with Hinduism. The *Svastika,* which is found represented as turning both to the right and to the left, has probably some religious significance and is certainly pre-Aryan.

We should also take note of a small bronze statuette with its arms quite covered with bracelets; the right one is bent towards the hip and the left supported on the knee. It is possibly an ancient nautch girl who has been dancing in worship of the Great Mother.

We have also a small statuette of steatite, with a stylized dress of a trefoil pattern, its eyes directed towards the tip of the nose. According to the Bhagavadgītā such was the attitude of the Yogin in trance and self-concentration, but some scholars have also thought of an old priest, perhaps the king-priest.

Several skeletons with trinkets have been found at Mohenjo Daro, sometimes also mere fragments of bones, together with broken clay-objects, pearls, arrows of flint and ivory, a spoon of shell, and so on. One might think of the later cult of relics.

But everywhere we are on unsafe ground, and we can only hope that future finds will throw light on what is yet uncertain.

# 4

# DOMINANT IDEAS IN THE FORMATION OF INDIAN CULTURE

## Franklin Edgerton

We turn now to a consideration of the religious and philosophical base of Indian culture, the essence of the civilization of the Indian subcontinent. We have before touched upon the variation in climate, daily life, language, and so on, that the subcontinent exhibits. Yet it must be emphasized that underlying this variety there is a strong unifying force that allows us to speak of Indian culture in the singular: the complex of custom and belief which shapes the lives of the vast majority of the inhabitants of the Indian subcontinent.

Nor are the ideas discussed by Professor Edgerton in this next selection exclusively "Hindu"; they are rather more truly Indian, a product of the total environment and the possession of the over-all culture rather than of a single religious group. For the principles of *Saṃsāra, karma* and *mokṣa*—Buddhist *nirvāṇa*—are at the center of all Indian religious systems. A Buddhist monk of the old Brotherhood of the Buddha's time and a Jain monk, equally with the Hindu ascetic, are following what Edgerton terms the *extraordinary* norm. Indeed, the three major religions of India (excluding Islam which is a latecomer and not within the scope of traditional India) can be said to differ more in detail than in substance.

With regard to Islam, it must be said (at the risk of offending some of my Muslim friends) that like the early Aryans, it has not escaped "Indianization." True, the Qur'ān, monolithic and unalterable, remains untouched and at the center of the religious world of some fifty million Muslims in the Republic of India (and another hundred thousand and more in Pakistan). Yet in their daily lives the Muslims of the subcontinent could not escape the influence of

Franklin Edgerton, "Dominant Ideas in the Formation of Indian Culture." From *Journal of the American Oriental Society,* Vol. 62 (1942), 151-56. Reprinted by permission of the author and the Americal Oriental Society.

*Indian* culture, and scholars can and do speak of "Indian Islam." Furthermore, one suspects that only in India could have arisen the Mughal emperor Akbar's somewhat syncretistic *din-e ilahi,* "religion of god" (note god with a small *g,* as opposed to Allah, "The God"). But Islam is beyond the scope of this volume; it has been brought in as a good example of the force and pervasiveness of the basic elements of Indian culture.

*Indian* culture is the norm of human life approved or accepted generally by the civilized inhabitants of India (Hindus) since roughly round about four or five hundred B.C. Its classical expression is found in literature from about that time on, in the Sanskrit, Pāli, and Prakrit languages, and later on in other languages, some Indo-Aryan, some Dravidian (especially Tamil and Telugu). It may properly be spoken of as approximately a unit in some important respects, and in most of these respects it is still the dominant cultural pattern over the greater part of India. It was, however, preceded by at least one earlier pattern of which we have a good deal of knowledge. I shall call this latter the Vedic culture. It was rather different from "Indian" culture in some of these important respects.

The word *formation* I take to mean historic origin.

In short, then, I shall suppose that I am asked to pick out words and phrases which, in my opinion, have been regarded by Indians since some centuries B.C. as specially important in their bearing on the conduct of human life, viewed as a norm; and to suggest how I think they were related to earlier words and phrases, or to the same words occurring in earlier phrases and perhaps bearing different meanings.

At the very outset, this quest is complicated by a striking dichotomy in Indian culture. There are two radically different norms of human life and conduct, both at least tolerated, indeed in some sense accepted and approved, each in its own sphere. I shall call them the *ordinary* and the *extraordinary* norms. One strange thing is that one of them seems to involve a complete negation or rejection of the other as an acceptable norm.

The first is the only one possible for the great mass of mankind, short of some future spiritual regeneration of the entire race. In this ordinary way of life, Hindu texts constantly speak of three broad aims, or aspects of the cultural norm, all of which are normal and acceptable, and which include everything that a normal man can, or at any rate ought to, aim at. These are, in Sanskrit, *dharma, artha,* and *kāma;* they are called the Group of Three, *trivarga.*

*Dharma* is propriety, socially approved conduct, in relation to one's fellow men or to other living beings (animals, or superhuman powers). Law, social usage, morality, and most of what we ordinarily mean by religion, all fall under this head.

*Artha* is profit, worldly advantage and success. It includes personal advancement in wealth, politics, business, professional and social activities of all sorts.

*Kāma* is love: success in dealing with the opposite sex.

In each of these three departments we have many extensive treatises called *śāstras,* at the same time practical and scientific (systematic) in character, and all treated with great respect as authoritative in their several fields. Their professed purpose is to lay down rules for successful prosecution of the aims of *dharma, artha,* or *kāma,* respectively. The field of *artha* is particularly varied; it includes all the professions, arts, and crafts, and in many of them special handbooks were composed. The theory is that man should, or at least may properly, cultivate all three—social propriety, worldly advantage, and love—but in a duly balanced way, so that activities in none of the three departments should violate the domains of the others. In actual practice, I know of no ground for supposing that people were apt to be reproached for overemphasis on *dharma;* while the *śāstras* or textbooks devoted to *artha* and *kāma,* especially the former, seem to us sometimes to recommend the violation of the precepts of *dharma.*

In this three-fold norm of Indian culture for the ordinary man, there is little that is startling to us in principle. Nor is there anything essentially new as compared with the older Vedic culture. Details of practice vary, naturally. Some peculiarly Indian institutions have left their mark. Thus the celebrated system of caste (*varṇa, jāti*)—originally merely a hardening, a rigid systematization, of occupational differences combined with rules of social intercourse, the like of which are found more or less all over the world—eventuated in a theory of quasi-biological differences inborn in men, which are supposed to make different men fitted by nature for different specific occupations and modes of life, which it is perilous to try to avoid. Even so great and independent a man as Gandhi still holds to this view, though he is careful to say that caste does not "confer privileges"; it only "prescribes duties."

It is more especially in approaching the other, "extraordinary" norm, that we must be prepared for surprises. The background of it involves some metaphysics, of a mild and simple sort.

Belief in some form of life after death is very common all over the world, and existed in Vedic culture, which was pre-"Indian" in the sense of my definition, though it was located in India. There, as commonly among ourselves, postmortal life was placed in some unearthly world or "heaven" (*svarga*). At least for the man who conformed to the approved cultural norm, it was expected that this life would be happy; nor does it appear that any end was assigned to it—at first. But in the later Vedic period of the texts called Brāhmaṇas, we begin to hear a great deal about "re-death," *punarmṛtyu,* which it was feared might end that postmortal life, and which people sought to avoid by religious or magical methods.

With the dawn of what I have defined as "Indian" culture, in the early Upaniṣads, this effort has come to be regarded as vain—for the ordinary man. Further, for him, life after death is now regarded as not different in nature, and not necessarily different even in location, from earthly life. Man is entangled in an indefinite series of lives, essentially like the present life, and ordinarily lived on this earth, though they may take place in some fancied other world. One may be reborn as an animal, as a man low or high in the social scale, even as a superhuman being, a *deva* (a "god" with a small initial letter—not to be confused with God; see below). But all such lives end in death, and are followed by other lives. It is an endless chain; the Sanskrit term is *saṃsāra,* "course, migration," and so "transmigration."

The relative excellence of any new birth is rigidly determined by the net balance of good and bad actions in previous births. This is the famous law of "karma" (Sanskrit *karman,* "action, deed"). It is a law of nature and works automatically; it is not administered by any God or superhuman agent. It is man's relation to propriety or morality, *dharma,* which alone determines. This provides a powerful drive in favor of *dharma* in the cultural pattern, tending to counterbalance the natural man's preference for the interests of *artha* and *kāma*. For more than two thousand years, it appears that almost all Hindus have regarded transmigration, determined by "karma," as an axiomatic fact. "By good deed a man becomes what is good; by evil deed, what is evil," as an early Upaniṣad puts it.

It might seem, indeed it has seemed to some Westerners, that this belief ought to have comforting and reassuring effects on those who hold it. It not only explains the ills of life as just results of past misdeeds, but further seems to make man master of his own future fate. If it leaves no room for divine mercy, it also never cuts off hope; there is no eternal hell, and the lowest being can rise to the status of a "god" (*deva*) simply by doing right.

But the attitude of thoughtful Hindus has been almost unanimously the opposite. They have regarded the chain of transmigration as a chain in the other sense, a bondage (*bandhana,* or a synonym). Even the life of a "god" is at any rate transitory. All pleasures come to an end; this knowledge poisons their enjoyment, and after they are gone their remembrance makes life doubly bitter. Death is an unavoidable misery, not less dread because it must be undergone over and over again; we saw that belief in, and fear of, "re-death" was older than the theory of rebirth. No human, at least, is free from disease, old age, separation from loved ones, and other ills. The fleeting pleasures of life by no means compensate for all these evils. In short, life is fundamentally bad (*dukha,* "misery"); that transmigration makes it inescapable means that we are imprisoned in an eternal dungeon.

Or is it necessarily eternal? Is there any way of cutting the Gordian knot of transmigration under "karma"?

For the ordinary man, say the Hindus, there is none. So long as one does nothing better than follow the pattern above described, performing various acts for the purposes of *dharma, artha,* and *kāma,* these acts must have their "fruit" or result (*phala*), good or bad, for the doer; and that (even the good act and its result) means continued existence in birth after birth. Since all births are evil, even the best and highest, which is the most that the ordinary man can hope for, is still evil.

There is, however, a possible way out. Few can attain it. It involves rejection of ordinary human aims; a denial, in theory at least complete, of the generally accepted cultural pattern. This is what I have called the *extraordinary* norm. In spite of variation in details of method, its several varieties agree substantially in the end to be sought, and in their attitude towards the ordinary way of life. And, significantly, its followers have received, even from those who cleave to that ordinary norm, the homage of reverence, implying a recognition of its superiority, though it may be regarded as unattainable by the generality of mankind.

We meet it first in the early Upaniṣads. Even before them in Vedic times, people sought freedom from death and other ills. And in later Vedic (Brāhmaṇa) times the favorite method was by *knowledge* (*jñāna, vidyā*), especially knowledge of the mystic, esoteric *identity* of the object of the quest with something under the control of the seeker. The possession of such knowledge conferred automatic, magic *control* over the end sought by the knower: "Knowledge is power," in a direct magical sense. This is a very ancient notion, clearly present in the oldest Vedic texts. I traced its relation to Upaniṣad thought in my presidential address before this Society, published in the *Journal* in 1929 (Vol. 49, pp. 97-121).

Seeking to control the entire universe and thus their own destiny, the Upaniṣad authors boldly declared that their own self (*ātman*), than which nothing could be more obviously under their control, was identical with the fundamental principle of the universe, most often called *brahman*. (The reasons for the choice of this term cannot be discussed here; see my article just mentioned.) One who *knew* this mystic truth (*ya evaṃ veda*) thereby *became* identical with the One, and so free from death and from any ill. By this knowledge of the supreme truth he automatically attained "freedom, release" (*mukti, mokṣa*) from the evils of mundane existence, especially from continued subjection to death. He possessed "immortality," *amṛtatva*.

In later times, different formulations of the supreme truth developed. And the somewhat crude magical theory became softened and refined; it came to be no longer felt as an operation of simple magic. But the fundamental way of controlling one's destiny continued to be *knowledge;* knowledge of the ultimate truth about the real nature of the world and of man's soul, his true self (*ātman,* or *puruṣa* "the man"). It was this, first and foremost, which gave release from the *saṃsāra,* transmigration, and from the effects of action, *karman.* Whoso knows is saved.

Even the earliest Upaniṣads stated the obvious corollary that the ordinary norm was unworthy, and its cultivation only painful in the end. "What is other than That is miserable," *ato 'anyad ārtam,* they said repeatedly. From this the inference was easy that the seeker for saving "knowledge" should completely renounce normal worldly life. Not only, they said, because it was worthless, but because it was distracting. It impeded the attainment of the higher goal by involving man in mundane interests. Thus arose the ideal norm of the wandering monk (*saṃnyāsin, bhikṣu*), the homeless ascetic, living on alms, cut off from family ties, possessions, and all worldly life. He stood outside of everything, even of caste; a member of any caste, or of none, might become a truth-seeking mendicant. All monks were brothers, and to them all was one. The truly enlightened man regards a learned brahman and a despised outcaste, a noble beeve or elephant and an unclean dog, as all one.

This supreme knowledge was only for the rare elect. Ascetic life (*tapas*) was popularly regarded as its outward sign, and sometimes confused with the inner reality, a fact of which hypocrites could and did take advantage to seek undeserved popular respect. At times the ascetic life, originally only ancillary to the search for knowledge, tended to obscure that goal, and to be thought of by the vulgar as the direct way to salvation. In later, but still fairly early times, other methods were cultivated as aids to enlightenment, and they too sometimes tended to displace it and to be thought of as primary ways of salvation. Noteworthy among these was devotion (*bhakti*) to a (usually) monotheistic and personal God (the usual term is *īśvara,* "the Lord"; not *deva,* "god"), often identified with Brahmā, a masculine, personalized form of the neuter Brahman, the originally impersonal First Principle of the universe. God's grace (*prasāda*) could grant salvation to his devotees as a reward for their personal devotion—originally, but later on not invariably, through the medium of a bestowal of the boon of true knowledge.

A still different aid to, or even substitute for, saving knowledge is taught in the celebrated Bhagavad Gītā. It points out that normal worldly action is motivated by desire or craving (*kāma, tṛṣṇā*). It is not what one does, but the motive of the act, that produces the binding effect of the law of karma. Accordingly, says this text, it is not at all necessary to renounce mundane life and activity, and adopt asceticism. All that is needed is to act with pure unselfishness, not caring what happens to oneself. Disinterested action, (*karma-*)*yoga* or "discipline" (in action), does not bind to continued rebirth. The Gītā is still the most popular religious authority in India, doubtless for this reason, that it allows salvation for the man who remains in worldly life, provided only that he is selfless.

But what is this salvation or "freedom" (*mokṣa*), the goal of the extraordinary cultural norm in all its forms, whatever their variant methods of seeking it? They all agree that it is complete and permanent freedom from transmigration, and from the law of *karma* which regulates it. That means freedom from life, or rather from empiric existence as we know it. The favorite term is *nirvāṇa,* occurring first in such texts as the Bhagavad Gītā and in Pāli Buddhist texts; the genuine Upaniṣads do not contain it, though they have roughly equivalent expressions. It, or the *Brahman* which is a semipersonalized expression for it, is sometimes defined as real (*sat;* not nonexistent), conscious (*cit;* not inert), and blissful (*ānanda*). Otherwise it is called "the supreme station (*parama pada*), than that which there is nothing better (*niḥśreyasa*)," or the like; or, in monotheistic texts, "becoming" or "going to God." Clearer positive descriptions hardly exist. It is utterly unlike existence as we know it—on a totally different plane. Indeed, at times the texts say that only negative statements about it are possible; *neti neti,* "No, no," a very old Upaniṣad says several times. All one can say is that anything one could say is false.

The word *nirvāṇa* means literally "extinction," as of a flame. It is not, however, extinction of existence; only of empiric existence as we know it. Originally, indeed, it seems to have meant extinction of the flames of desire, which is often compared to a consuming fire, and which leads to action, which leads to continued rebirth. It is therefore their "extinction" which constitutes salvation (*mukti, mokṣa*), the goal of the extraordinary norm.

Note that morality, or even morality combined with traditional religious observances (*dharma*), does not lead to this goal. Herein lies a great difference between Hindu and Western cultural norms. In the West there is no such dichotomy. Here relatively few people retire from the world to live religious lives; but even if they do, their aim and their ideal remain essentially the same as those which are enjoined on the ordinary man who would live virtuously. In India, not only *artha* and *kāma,* but even *dharma* exists primarily for the ordinary norm only. To the seeker of salvation, it is important at most in early stages. The morally impure cannot, of course, even begin the hard quest. But when the goal is reached, one is beyond good and evil. For him there is nothing to do, good or bad.

Yet in spite of this sharp distinction, the profound (if often uncomprehending) veneration which ordinary Hindus seem usually to have felt for the rare exponents of the extraordinary norm can hardly have failed to have some effect on their lives. Even if I had the time, I could not attempt a full discussion of this question. But before closing I should like to mention a single feature of Hindu practical morality, a very important one, which seems to me to owe much to the influence of the extraordinary norm.

The "Golden Rule," that one ought to treat others like oneself, is as important in Hindu ethics as in Christianity. It is even carried farther, for it applies to animals (which like men are involved in transmigration under "karma"). It is summed up in the doctrine of *ahiṃsā,* "no injury" to any living being.

Now in Christianity this doctrine rests, so far as I can see, simply on its natural appeal to thoughtful men. In Hinduism it has a metaphysical background; it is a logical deduction from the Upaniṣad doctrine mentioned above (which has always been widely accepted in India), that the soul or real self of every man is identical with that of the universe (*tat tvam asi,* "That art thou"). It follows, since things which are equal to the same thing are equal to each other, that one must identify his own self with all other selves. If he harms others, he harms himself. The Golden Rule is thus proved, in a logically irrefutable way, if you accept the premises. That is why the supremely moral man, even while he lives by the ordinary norm, "identifies his self with the self of all being" (*sarvabhūtātmabhūtātman,* as the Gītā says), and "delights in the welfare of all beings" (*sarvabhūtāhite ratāḥ*).

# 5

# HISTORY OF INDIAN THOUGHT


## Sarvepalli Radhakrishnan and Charles A. Moore


This remarkably concise and succinct summation of the main elements of Indian thought requires little comment from an editor; it speaks for itself. I would only point out that again we are dealing with "Indian" thought, rather than with Hindu, Jain, or any other more narrowly sectarian stream of thought.

Worth noting is the role of knowledge, *vidyā,* and of intuition in Indian religion and philosophy. The second of the Four Noble Truths of Buddhism is that the suffering of this world is the result of *avidyā,* "nonknowledge" or ignorance. Further, the intuitive grasp of reality is at the basis of the Zen *satori,* which I once heard Alan Watts—certainly one of the most articulate interpreters of Zen Buddhism in the United States—describe as the sudden and perhaps momentary realization that everything is exactly as it should be—a realization of complete cosmic harmony. Zen Buddhism, incidentally, though primarily identified with Japan (and much in vogue these days) has its roots, through China, in India. The word "zen" goes back to Sanskrit *dhyāna* "meditation."

Dr. Sarvepalli Radhakrishnan is the second (and present) president of India. Whether there is a moral to be got from the fact, I do not know.

At the very outset, it should be emphasized that Indian philosophy has had an extremely long and complex development, much more complex than is usually realized, and probably a longer history of continuous development than any other philosophical tradition. While the historical perspective is undoubtedly of immense importance in the study of such a tradition, it is impossible to present an exact historical survey of this development. Because of the Indians' lack of concern for chronology, many of the details of the chronological sequence of the writings either are lost or no record of them was kept. In a sense, the history of Indian philosophy can be written, if only in broadest outline, but no history of philosophy can be complete without some acquaintance with the philosophers who were responsible for the doctrines and for the development of thought. However, so unhistorical, or perhaps so deeply philosophical, was the nature of the ancient Indians that much more is known about the philosophies than about the philosophers. Relatively few of the great philosophers of ancient Indian thought are known to us and some of the most famous names to which history attributes certain philosophical doctrines or systems are now admitted to be legendary. On the one hand, we are occasionally aware of the author of some doctrines but, as in the case of Indian materialism and some other movements, original texts are not available and the details of the systems are completely unknown.

In broad outline, Indian philosophy may be said to have had four major periods of development up to the time of its serious decline about A.D. 1700. The Vedic period is dimmed by obscurity, but it may be placed approximately between 2500 and 600 B.C. This is the period during which the Āryans, having come down into India from central Asia, settled their new homeland and gradually expanded and developed their Āryan culture and civilization. In the technical sense of the term, this can hardly be called a philosophical age. It is to be thought of as an age of groping, in which religion, philosophy, superstition, and thought were inextricably interrelated and yet in perpetual conflict. It is an age of philosophical development, however, and its culminating doctrines, those expounded in the major Upaniṣads, have determined the tone if not the precise pattern of the Indian philosophical development ever since.

The literature of this period consists of the four Vedas (*Ṛg Veda, Yajur Veda, Sāma Veda,* and *Atharva Veda*), each of which has four parts, known as Mantras, Brāhmaṇas, Āraṇyakas, and Upaniṣads. The Mantras (hymns), especially the later ones in the *Ṛg Veda,* constitute the actual beginning of Indian philosophy. By progressing from the not unusual polytheism of the early Vedas, through monotheism, to suggestions of monism, these poems and songs paved the way for the monistic tendencies of the Upaniṣads.

The Brāhmaṇas are chiefly religious documents, including ritualistic precepts and sacrificial duties. The Āraṇyakas and the Upaniṣads constitute the concluding parts of the Brāhmaṇas, and in these philosophical problems are discussed. The Brāhmaṇas provide the ritual to be observed by the householder, but when the householder has reached old age, he resorts to the forest and needs a substitute for the ritual he has known as a householder. The Āraṇyakas, which come between the Brāhmaṇas and the Upaniṣads, supply this need by encouraging meditation for those who live in the forest. The Āraṇyakas form the transition link between the ritual of the Brāhmaṇas and the philosophy of the Upaniṣads. While the hymns are the creation of poets, the Brāhmaṇas are the work of priests, and the Upaniṣads are the meditations of philosophers. The Upaniṣads, though in one sense a continuation of the Vedic religion, are in another sense a strong philosophical protest against the religion of the Brāhmaṇas. It is in the Upaniṣads that the tendency to spiritual monism, which in one form or another characterizes much of Indian philosophy, was first established and where intuition rather than reason was first recognized as the true guide to ultimate truth.

The second period of philosophical development is the Epic Period, dated approximately from 500 or 600 B.C. to A.D. 200. This period is characterized by the indirect presentation of philosophical doctrines through the medium of nonsystematic and nontechnical literature, especially the great epics, the *Rāmāyaṇa* and the *Mahābhārata*. In addition, however, the period includes the rise and early development of Buddhism, Jainism, Śaivism, and Vaiṣṇavism. The *Bhagavad-gītā,* which is a part of the *Mahābhārata,* ranks as one of the three most authoritative texts in Indian philosophical literature. Furthermore, the beginnings of the orthodox schools of Indian philosophy also belong to this period. Most of the systems had their beginnings about the time of the rise of Buddhism, and developed side by side for centuries. The systematic works of the major schools were written later, but the origin of the doctrines of the several schools most probably occurred during the Epic Period. This was one of the most fertile periods of philosophy in India as well as in several other parts of the world—Greece, China, Persia, and elsewhere. A great amount of philosophical or semiphilosophical material was produced during the period, and it is very probable that our knowledge of the doctrines developed at that time merely scratches the surface of the wealth, depth, and variety of philosophical speculation that took place. It was during this period that such philosophies as skepticism, naturalism, materialism, and so forth, arose along with the other heterodox systems of Buddhism and Jainism and what were later known as the orthodox systems of Hinduism. It is out of this wealth of material that the later systems—the orthodox systems of Hinduism and the unorthodox systems of Cārvāka, Buddhism, and Jainism—were perforce brought into clearer perspective by the construction of systematic treatises.

It was also during this period that many of the Dharmaśāstras, treatises on ethical and social philosophy, were compiled. These, like the rest of the philosophical texts of the period, are classed as *smṛtis*—that is, traditional texts, as contrasted with the literature of the Vedic Period, which is known as *śruti,* revealed scriptures or authoritative texts. The Dharmaśāstras are systematic treatises concerning the conduct of life among the Āryans, describing their social organization and their ethical and religious functions and obligations.

The third period is the *Sūtra* Period, which is dated approximately from the early centuries of the Christian era. In this period the systematic treatises of the various schools were written and the systems took the basic form they were to preserve henceforth. The doctrines of each of the systems were presented in orderly, systematic, and logically developed sets of aphorisms, extremely brief, sometimes enigmatic, statements which, according to some interpretations, are merely reminders for the initiated to enable them to recall the details of philosophical systems to which they belonged and whose fuller doctrines were known only to those within the fold of the system. During this period the critical attitude in philosophy was distinctly developed along with the systematic, and the *Sūtras* themselves contain not only the positive developments of the systems but also keen and comprehensive polemics against opposing systems. Whereas during the preceding period philosophical thought and discussion had their origin, they were at that time carried on at the precritical level. In the *Sūtras,* however, we have self-conscious thought and reflection and no longer merely constructive imagination and spontaneous insights.

The six Hindu systems presented in *sūtra* form during this period are the Nyāya or logical realism; the Vaiśeṣika or realistic pluralism; the Sāṃkhya or evolutionary dualism; the Yoga or disciplined meditation; the Pūrva Mīmāṃsā or earlier interpretative investigations of the Vedas, relating to conduct; and the Uttara Mīmāṃsā or later investigations of the Vedas, relating to knowledge, also called Vedānta, the "end of the Vedas."

The fourth period, the Scholastic Period, is that in which commentaries were written upon the *Sūtras* in order to explain them. Without elaboration and explanation the *Sūtras* are almost unintelligible. Not only were commentaries written upon the *sūtras,* but also commentaries upon commentaries, and commentaries upon these, almost without limit. It is impossible to provide dates for this period with any degree of certainty. It is generally dated from the *Sūtra* Period to the seventeenth century. The literature of this period is primarily explanatory, but is also strongly and sometimes grossly polemical. There is a brood of "Schoolmen," noisy controversialists, indulging in oversubtle theories and finespun arguments, who fought fiercely over details of philosophical doctrines and who were in constant philosophical conflict with representatives of other schools. Sometimes the commentaries are more confusing than enlightening. Instead of clear explanation and thought, one often finds mere words; instead of philosophy, logic-chopping. Obscurity of thought, subtlety of logic, and intolerance of opposition are marks of the worst types of commentators. The better types, however, are invaluable and are respected almost as much as the creators of the systems themselves. Śaṃkara, for example, the writer of a famous commentary on the *Sūtra* of the Vedānta system, is thought of more highly as a philosopher than is Bādarāyaṇa, the seer who wrote the original *Vedānta Sūtra* (also called the *Brahma Sūtra*). The Scholastic Period is one of explanation of the original *Sūtras,* but, like any scholastic period, it has also produced quibbling and unphilosophical debates which are relatively worthless. On the other hand, it has brought forth some of the greatest of all Indian philosophers. Among these, in addition to Śaṃkara, are Kumārila, Śrīdhara, Rāmānuja, Madhva, Vācaspati, Udayana, Bhāskara, Jayanta, Vijñānabhikṣu, and Raghunātha. These great thinkers have been much more than commentators on ancient systems, although, in their modesty, they have claimed to be no more. In fact, however, they have been, to all intents and purposes, creators of their own systems. In the guise of commentators, they have elaborated points of view which, though capable of being related to the original system of which they are supposed to be commentaries, are new expositions rather than mere explanations. For example, the three major forms of Vedānta, those developed by Śaṃkara, Rāmānuja, and Madhva, are distinct and elaborate systems, although they all stem from the same *Vedānta Sūtra* of Bādarāyaṇa. This type of development is indicative of the unique way in which Indian philosophers have maintained their traditional respect for the past and their recognition of the value of authority in philosophy, but, without seeming to break this tradition, have also carried along the free development of thought as their insight and reason directed.

While, in a sense, the Scholastic Period is still in progress, since interpretations of ancient ideas and systems are still being written, Indian philosophy lost its dynamic spirit about the sixteenth century when India became the victim of outside powers. First the Moslems and then the British assumed control of the country, not only physically but also in the realm of thought. The Moslems undermined Āryan culture and thought as far as possible, and the British, in their time, did as much as they could to belittle the thought of traditional India. For a long time, the English-educated Indians were apparently ashamed of their own philosophical tradition, and it became the mark of intelligence as well as expediency to be as European and as English in thought and in life as possible. While the coming of the British brought about a revival in education, the resulting revival of Indian thought was unintentional, to say the least. During this period indigenous reform movements like that of the Brāhmo Samāj and the Ārya Samāj took a leading part in India's philosophical and religious renaissance. More recently, especially since the nationalist movement began, and more especially since the re-establishment of India as a free and independent nation, the revival of Indian philosophy as such and the consciousness of the greatness of India's philosophical past have been most prominent developments in the field. During the twentieth century, the Indian mind has been affected by the Western, but the Western mind has also been influenced by the Indian more than ever before, through the writings of contemporary poets, sages, and philosophers. To be sure, the revival of the Indian consciousness of the greatness of its own philosophical past has tended in recent years to develop a nationalistic tone in philosophy as well as in politics. The resulting tendency of extremists to minimize or reject the revival and development of philosophy which was effected by the contact of Indians and Westerners has not been a healthy sign. We of today are able to see further than our predecessors, since we have climbed on their shoulders. Instead, therefore, of resting content with the foundations so nobly laid in the past, we must build in harmony with ancient endeavor as well as with contemporary thought. The future development of Indian philosophy, if one may hazard a guess, will be in terms of a more synthetic approach to Indian and Western points of view.

## THE SPIRIT OF INDIAN PHILOSOPHY

Indian philosophy, it has been noted, is extremely complex. Through the ages the Indian philosophical mind has probed deeply into many aspects of human experience and the external world. Although some methods, such as the experimental method of modern science, have been relatively less prominent than others, not only the problems of Indian philosophy but also the methods used and the conclusions reached in the pursuit of truth have certainly been as far-reaching in their extent, variety, and depth as those of other philosophical traditions. The six basic systems and the many subsystems of Hinduism, the four chief schools of Buddhism, the two schools of Jainism, and the materialism of the Cārvāka are evidence enough of the diversity of views in Indian philosophy. The variety of the Indian perspective is unquestionable. Accordingly, it is very difficult to cite any specific doctrines or methods as characteristic of Indian philosophy as a whole and applicable to all the multitudinous systems and subsystems developed through nearly four millenniums of Indian philosophical speculation.

Nevertheless, in certain respects there is what might be called a distinct spirit of Indian philosophy. This is exemplified by certain attitudes which are fairly characteristic of the Indian philosophical mind or which stand as points of view that have been emphasized characteristically by Indians in their philosophies.

(1) The chief mark of Indian philosophy in general is its concentration upon the spiritual. Both in life and in philosophy the spiritual motive is predominant in India. Except for the relatively minor materialistic school of the Cārvāka and related doctrines, philosophy in India conceives man to be spiritual in nature, interested primarily in his spiritual destiny, and relates him in one way or another to a universe which is also spiritual in essential character. Neither man nor the universe is looked upon as physical in essence, and material welfare is never recognized as the goal of human life, except by the Cārvāka. Philosophy and religion are intimately related because philosophy itself is regarded as a spiritual adventure,

and also because the motivation both in philosophy and in religion concerns the spiritual way of life in the here-and-now and the eventual spiritual salvation of man in relation to the universe. Practically all of Indian philosophy, from its beginning in the Vedas to the present day, has striven to bring about a socio-spiritual reform in the country, and philosophical literature has taken many forms—mythological, popular, or technical, as the circumstances required—in order to promote such spiritual life. The problems of religion have always given depth and power and purpose to the Indian philosophical mind and spirit.

(2) Another characteristic view of Indian philosophy is the belief in the intimate relationship of philosophy and life. This attitude of the practical application of philosophy to life is found in every school of Indian philosophy. While natural abundance and material prosperity paved the way for the rise of philosophical speculation, philosophy has never been considered a mere intellectual exercise. The close relationship between theory and practice, doctrine and life, has always been outstanding in Indian thought. Every Indian system seeks the truth, not as academic "knowledge for its own sake," but to learn the truth which shall make men free. This is not, as it has been called, the modern pragmatic attitude. It is much larger and much deeper than that. It is not the view that truth is measured in terms of the practical, but rather that the truth is the only sound guide for practice, that truth alone has efficacy as a guide for man in his search for salvation. Every major system of Indian philosophy takes its beginnings from the practical and tragic problems of life and searches for the truth in order to solve the problem of man's distress in the world in which he finds himself. There has been no teaching which remained a mere word of mouth or dogma of schools. Every doctrine has been turned into a passionate conviction, stirring the heart of man and quickening his breath, and completely transforming his personal nature. In India, philosophy is for life; it is to be lived. It is not enough to *know* the truth; the truth must be *lived*. The goal of the Indian is not to know the ultimate truth but to *realize* it, to become one with it.

Another aspect of the intimate inseparability of theory and practice, philosophy and life, in Indian philosophy is to be found in the universally prevalent demand for moral purification as an imperative preliminary for the would-be student of philosophy or searcher after truth. Śaṃkara's classic statement of this demand calls for a knowledge of the distinction between the eternal and the non-eternal—that is, a questioning tendency in the inquirer; the subjugation of all desire for the fruits of action either in this life or in a hereafter, a renunciation of all petty desire, personal motive, and practical interest; tranquillity, self-control, renunciation, patience, peace of mind, and faith; a desire for release (*mokṣa*) as the supreme goal of life.

(3) Indian philosophy is characterized by the introspective attitude and the introspective approach to reality. Philosophy is thought of as *ātmavidyā,* knowledge of the self. Philosophy can start either with the external world or with the internal world of man's inner nature, the self of man. In its pursuit of truth, Indian philosophy has always been strongly dominated by concern with the inner life and self of man rather than the external world of physical nature. Physical science, though developed extensively in the Golden Age of Indian culture, was never considered the road to ultimate truth; truth is to be sought and found within. The subjective, then, rather than the objective, becomes the focus of interest in Indian philosophy, and, therefore, psychology and ethics are considered more important as aspects or branches of philosophy than the sciences which study physical nature. This is not to say that the Indian mind has not studied the physical world; in fact, on the contrary, India's achievements in the realm of positive science were at one time truly outstanding, especially in the mathematical sciences such as algebra, astronomy, and geometry, and in the applications of these basic sciences to numerous phases of human activity. Zoology, botany, medicine, and related sciences have also been extremely prominent in Indian thought. Be this as it may, the Indian, from time immemorial, has felt that the inner spirit of man is the most significant clue to his reality and to that of the universe, more significant by far than the physical or the external.

(4) This introspective interest is highly conducive to idealism, of course, and consequently most Indian philosophy is idealistic in one form or another. The tendency of Indian philosophy, especially Hinduism, has been in the direction of monistic idealism. Almost all Indian philosophy believes that reality is *ultimately* one and *ultimately* spiritual. Some systems have seemed to espouse dualism or pluralism, but even these have been deeply permeated by a strong monistic character. If we concentrate our attention upon the underlying spirit of Indian philosophy rather than its variety of opinions, we shall find that this spirit is embodied in the tendency to interpret life and reality in the way of monistic idealism. This rather unusual

attitude is attributable to the nonrigidity of the Indian mind and to the fact that the attitude of monistic idealism is so plastic and dynamic that it takes many forms and expresses itself even in seemingly conflicting doctrines. These are not conflicting doctrines in fact, however, but merely different expressions of an underlying conviction which provides basic unity to Indian philosophy as a whole.

Materialism undoubtedly had its day in India, and, according to sporadic records and constant and determined efforts on the part of other systems to denounce it, the doctrine apparently enjoyed widespread acceptance at one time. Nevertheless, materialism could not hold its own; its adherents have been few in number, and its positive influence has been negligible. Indian philosophy has not been oblivious to materialism; rather, it has known it, has overcome it, and has accepted idealism as the only tenable view, whatever specific form that idealism might take.

(5) Indian philosophy makes unquestioned and extensive use of reason, but intuition is accepted as the only method through which the ultimate can be known. Reason, intellectual knowledge, is not enough. Reason is not useless or fallacious, but it is insufficient. To know reality one must have an actual experience of it. One does not merely *know* the truth in Indian philosophy; one *realizes* it. The word which most aptly describes philosophy in India is *darśana,* which comes from the verbal root *dṛś,* meaning "to see." "To see" is to have a direct intuitive experience of the object, or, rather, to realize it in the sense of becoming one with it. No complete knowledge is possible as long as there is the relationship of the subject on the one hand and the object on the other. Later developments in Indian philosophy, from the time of the beginning of the systems, have all depended in large part upon reason for the systematic formulation of doctrines and systems, for rational demonstration or justification, and in polemical conflicts of system against system. Nevertheless, all the systems, except the Cārvāka, agree that there is a higher way of knowing reality, beyond the reach of reason—namely, the direct perception or experience of the ultimate reality, which cannot be known by reason in any of its forms. Reason can demonstrate the truth, but reason cannot discover or reach the truth. While reason may be the method of philosophy in its more intellectualistic sense, intuition is the only method of comprehending the ultimate. Indian philosophy is thus characterized by an ultimate dependence upon intuition, along with

the recognition of the efficacy of reason and intellect when applied in their limited capacity and with their proper function.

(6) Another characteristic of Indian philosophy, one which is closely related to the preceding one, is its so-called acceptance of authority. Although the systems of Indian philosophy vary in the degree to which they are specifically related to the ancient *śruti,* not one of the systems—orthodox or unorthodox, except the Cārvāka—openly stands in violation of the accepted intuitive insights of its ancient seers, whether it be the Hindu seers of the Upaniṣads, the intuitive experience of the Buddha, or the similarly intuitive wisdom of Mahāvīra, the founder of Jainism, as we have it today. Indian philosophers have always been conscious of tradition and, as has been indicated before, the great system-builders of later periods claimed to be merely commentators, explaining the traditional wisdom of the past. While the specific doctrines of the past may be changed by interpretation, the general spirit and frequently the basic concepts are retained from age to age. Reverence for authority does not militate against progress, but it does lend a unity of spirit by providing a continuity of thought which has rendered philosophy especially significant in Indian life and solidly unified against any philosophical attitude contradicting its basic characteristics of spirituality, inwardness, intuition, and the strong belief that the truth is to be lived, not merely known.

The charge of indulging in an exaggerated respect for authority may be legitimately leveled against some of Indian philosophy, but this respect for the past is rooted in the deep conviction that those who really know reality are those who have *realized* the truth and that it is to them that we must turn ultimately, beyond all our power of reasoning, if we are to attain any comprehension of the truth which they saw and realized. As has been said, India has produced a great variety of philosophical doctrines and systems. This has been true despite universal reverence for and acceptance of the authority of the ancient seers as the true discoverers of wisdom. The variety of the systems, even in their basic conceptions, looked at in the light of the prevalent acceptance of authority, reveals the fact that this reverence has not made Indian philosophy a dogmatic religious creed, as is often alleged, but rather a single tone or trend of thought on basic issues. How completely free from traditional bias the systems are is seen, for example, by the fact that the original Sāṃkhya says nothing about the possible existence of God, although it is emphatic in its doctrine of the theoretical undemonstrability of his existence; the Vaiśeṣika and the Yoga, especially the latter, admit the existence of God, but do not consider him to be the creator of the universe; the Mīmāṃsā speaks of God but denies his importance and efficacy in the moral ordering of the world. To emphasize the point further, reference should be made also to the early Buddhist systems, which reject God, and to the Cārvākas, who deny God without qualification.

(7) Finally, there is the over-all synthetic tradition which is essential to the spirit and method of Indian philosophy. This is as old as the *Ṛg Veda,* where the seers realized that true religion comprehends all religions, so that "God is one but men call him by many names." Indian philosophy is clearly characterized by the synthetic approach to the various aspects of experience and reality. Religion and philosophy, knowledge and conduct, intuition and reason, man and nature, God and man, noumenon and phenomena, are all brought into harmony by the synthesizing tendency of the Indian mind. The Hindu is prone to believe even that all the six systems, as well as their varieties of subsystems, are in harmony with one another—in fact, that they complement one another in the total vision, which is one. As contrasted with Western philosophy, with its analytic approach to reality and experience, Indian philosophy is fundamentally synthetic. The basic texts of Indian philosophy treat not only one phase of experience and reality, but the full content of the philosophic sphere. Metaphysics, epistemology, ethics, religion, psychology, facts, and value are not cut off one from the other but are treated in their natural unity as aspects of one life and experience or of a single comprehensive reality.

It is this synthetic vision of Indian philosophy which has made possible the intellectual and religious tolerance which has become so pronounced in Indian thought and in the Indian mind throughout the ages. Recent squabbles between religious communities, bred of new political factionalism, are not outgrowths of the Indian mind but, instead, are antagonistic to its unique genius for adaptability and tolerance, which takes all groups and all communities into its one truth and one life.

In addition to these general characteristics of Indian philosophy from the intellectual or theoretical point of view, there is also a fundamental unity of perspective in the practical realm. This has several aspects. In the first place, there is the fact, mentioned earlier, that all philosophies in India—Hindu, Buddhist, Jaina, and Cārvāka—have a practical motivation, stemming from man's practical problems of life, his limitations and suffering, and culminating in every case except the Cārvāka in a consideration of his ultimate liberation. In every case, including the Cārvāka, the motivation is practical rather than theoretical, for the Cārvāka is interested, not in theory for its own sake, but in living a life of pleasure since it believes the world is conducive to that type of life and justifies no other. The goal of life in Hinduism, Buddhism, and Jainism is essentially the same. *Mokṣa* (liberation) is the ultimate objective for Hinduism and Jainism, and *nirvāṇa* is the goal in Buddhism. The precise meanings of liberation vary among the different schools, even among those within the framework of Buddhism and Hinduism, but the essential meaning of both *mokṣa* and *nirvāṇa* is emancipation or liberation from turmoil and suffering and freedom from rebirth. In some instances, the goal seems to be negative, consisting essentially of freedom from pain and freedom from rebirth, but in reality it is the positive achievement of a richer and fuller life and the attainment of infinite bliss. The spirit re-achieves its original purity, sometimes by becoming identical with the Absolute, sometimes by a life of communion with God, sometimes simply by the eternal existence of the pure spirit in its individuality, but in all cases free from the limitations and entanglements of life.

The several schools and systems of Indian philosophy are of one mind not only with reference to the goal of life, but also with reference to the good life on earth. The essential spirit of the philosophy of life of Hinduism, Buddhism, and Jainism is that of nonattachment. This is an attitude of mind with which the individual fulfills his part in life and lives a "normal" everyday existence in company with his fellow men, without being entangled in or emotionally disturbed by the results of his actions. He attains a mental and spiritual superiority to worldly values and is never enslaved by them. This is not negativism or escapism, for one takes part in everyday activities in accordance with his place in society. However, it is living and acting without any sense of attachment to the things of this world and without any selfishness whatsoever.

Hinduism, Buddhism, and Jainism, in all their branches, also accept the underlying doctrines of *karma* and rebirth. All of these schools believe that man must be morally and spiritually perfected before he can attain salvation. They also believe that justice is the law of the moral life exactly as cause-and-effect is the law of the natural world. What one sows, one must reap. Since justice and moral and spiritual perfection are not achievable in one life, all these systems believe in rebirth, so as to provide an opportunity for moral progress and eventual perfection. Throughout Indian philosophy, from the earliest Vedas to the latest developments, the moral order of the universe has been an accepted doctrine of all Indian thinkers except the Cārvākas. *Karma* and rebirth are the instrumentalities by which the moral order of the universe is worked out in the life of man.

There is a further common element which unifies schools of Hindu philosophy in the practical realm, although the heterodox schools—the Cārvāka, Buddhism, and Jainism—do not conform to this pattern. The way of life accepted by all schools of Hinduism, regardless of metaphysical and epistemological variations, includes the fourfold division of society, the four stages of life, and the four basic values which man seeks. In Hinduism, society is divided into four groups (*varṇa,* frequently translated as castes) determined generally according to occupational ability—namely, the priest-teacher (*brāhmin*), the king or political and military leader (*kṣatriya*), the merchant (*vaiśya*), and the laborer (*śūdra*). The first three of these are called the twice-born—that is, they are religiously initiated Hindus—whereas the *śūdras* are not so accepted. The lives of the twice-born are to consist of the four stages of the student (*brahmacārin*), the householder (*gṛhastha*), the forest-dweller (*vānaprastha*), and the wandering monk (*sannyāsin* or *saṃnyāsin*). In this social scheme, one does not enter the life of asceticism until after he has fulfilled his obligations to his fellow man as a student and as a householder, but in the later stages of life one is to concentrate more and more upon the spiritual and upon his search for liberation. The goals of life which are accepted by all Hindus are righteousness or obedience to the moral law (*dharma*), wealth or material welfare (*artha*), pleasure (*kāma*), and emancipation (*mokṣa*). *Dharma* prevails throughout life; that is, neither pleasure nor wealth is to be obtained through violation of the rules of morality. *Mokṣa* is the ultimate goal to which all men should aspire. This social philosophy is accepted without question by all Hindus. It is presented in the literature of the Dharmaśāstras, but is not found in any elaboration or with any philosophical justification in the basic technical philosophical texts. This common ideal life of all Hindus provides a spirit of unity to the social and moral life of the country, although Buddhists and Jainas, who are greatly in the minority, do not follow the same specific pattern of life.

# 6

# THE ORIGINS OF HINDU SPECULATION


## Franklin Edgerton


The next three selections are specifically Hindu rather than Indian; yet their relevance to the total Indian culture beyond Hinduism—especially the first of the selections—cannot be minimized. That we speak of "orthodox" Hinduism and the "heterodox" systems of Buddhism and Jainism implies perhaps more than it should. The important fact of the speculation that marks the beginning of the traditional period lies in the speculation *per se,* in general terms, as an Indian phenomenon, without qualification as to Hindu, Buddhist, or Jain. It must be stressed that the three main systems, the orthodox Hinduism and the heterodox Buddhism and Jainism, have their roots in the same period, in the common *Indian* restlessness and speculation.

There is little doubt that it was a reaction against the priest-ridden (brahmin) ritualism of the end of the Vedic or Brahmanical period (Aryan, but pre-Indian in Edgerton's view) that led to the ferment and (philosophic) unease and dissatisfaction of the seventh century B.C. The two "heterodox" systems and the "orthodox" have, in essence, probably more in common than any one of them—including Hinduism—has with the ritualism of the preceding period. They have in common many elements, as has been pointed out, and they seem to be equally strong in their reaction to and rejection of the brahmanism or priestly domination that marks the preceding period. That one system is "orthodox" and the other two termed "heterodox" is simply that Hinduism accepts and accommodates itself to the authority of the Vedas while the other two systems do not, specifically rejecting much—caste, for instance—that Hinduism accepts. Yet even in the Bhagavad Gītā, one of the central documents of Hinduism, the Vedas are at one point said to be as nought compared with devotion to God, *bhakti,* in the quest for *mokṣa,* or release from the cycle of birth and rebirth.

The records of Hindu religious thought, as of Hindu literature in general, begin with the Rig Veda. This is a collection consisting mostly of hymns of praise and prayer to a group of deities who are primarily personified powers of nature—sun, fire, wind, sky, and the like—with the addition of some gods whose original nature is obscure. The religion represented by the Rig Veda, however, is by no means a simple or primitive nature-worship. Before the dawn of history it had developed into a ritualistic cult, a complicated system of sacrifices, the performance of which was the class privilege of a guild of priests. In the hands of this priestly class the sacrificial cult became more and more elaborate, and occupied more and more the center of the stage. At first merely a means of gratification and propitiation of the gods, the sacrifice gradually became an end in itself and finally, in the period succeeding the hymns of the Rig Veda, the gods became supernumeraries. The now all-important sacrifices no longer persuaded, but compelled them to do what the sacrificer desired; or else, at times, the sacrifice produced the desired result immediately, without any participation whatsoever on the part of the gods. The gods are even spoken of themselves as offering sacrifices; and it is said that they owe their divine position, or their very existence, to the sacrifice. This extreme glorification of the ritual performance appears in the period of the Brāhmaṇas, theological textbooks whose purpose is to expound the mystic meaning of the various rites. They are later in date than the Rig-Vedic hymns; and their religion, a pure magical ritualism, is the apotheosis, or the *reductio ad absurdum,* of the ritualistic nature-worship of the hymns.

Even in Rig-Vedic times the priestly ritual was so elaborate, and so expensive, that in the nature of things only rich men, mainly princes, could engage in it. It was therefore not only a hieratic but an aristocratic cult. The real religion of the great mass of the people was diffierent. We find it portrayed best in the Atharva Veda. This is a collection of hymns or rather magic charms, intended to accompany a mass of simpler rites and ceremonies which were not connected with the hieratic cult of the Rig Veda. Almost every conceivable human need and aspiration is represented by these popular performances. Their religious basis may be described as primitive animism, and their method of operation as simple magic. That is, they regard all creatures, things, powers, and even abstract principles, as volitional potencies or "spirits," or as animated by "spirits," which they seek to control by incantations and magic rites. They know also the higher gods of the Rig-Vedic pantheon, and likewise other gods which perhaps belonged at the start to aboriginal, non-"Aryan" tribes ("Aryan" is the name which the Vedic Hindus apply to themselves). But they invoke these gods after the manner of magic-mongers, much as medieval European incantations invoke the persons of the Trinity and Christian saints in connection with magic practices to heal a broken bone or to bring rain for the crops.

Later Hindu thought developed primarily out of the hieratic, Rig-Vedic religion; but it contains also quite a dash of lower, more popular beliefs. The separation of the two elements is by no means always easy. The truth seems to be that the speculations out of which the later forms of thought developed were carried on mainly by priests, adherents of the hieratic ritual religion. Almost all the intellectual leaders of the community belonged to the priestly class. But they were naturally—almost inevitably—influenced by the popular religion which surrounded them. Indeed, there was no opposition between the two types of religion, nor such a cleavage as our description may suggest. The followers of the hieratic cult also engaged in the practices that belonged to the more popular religion. This accounts for the constant infiltration from the "lower" sphere into the "higher," which we see going on at all periods. At times it is hard to decide whether a given new development is due to the intrusion of popular beliefs, or to internal evolution within the sphere of the priestly religion itself.

For we can clearly see the growth of certain new views within the Rig Veda itself. Out of the older ritualistic nature-worship, with its indefinite plurality of gods, arises in many Rig-Vedic hymns a new attitude, a sort of mitigated polytheism, to which has been given the name of *henotheism*. By this is meant a religious point of view which, when dealing for the moment with any particular god, seems to feel it is an insult to his dignity to admit the competition of other deities. And so, either the particular god of the moment is made to absorb all the others, who are declared to be manifestations of him; or else, he is given attributes which in strict logic could only be given to a sole monotheistic deity. Thus various Vedic gods are each at different times declared to be the creator, preserver, and animator of the universe, the sole ruler of all creatures, human and divine, and so on. Such hymns, considered separately, seem clearly to imply monotheism; but all that they really imply is a ritualistic henotheism. As each god comes upon the stage in the procession of rites, he is impartially granted this increasingly extravagant praise, until everything that could be said of all the gods collectively is said of each of them in turn, individually. We see that Vedic henotheism is rooted in the hieratic ritual, without which it perhaps would hardly have developed.

But it was not long before some advanced thinkers saw that such things as the creation of the world and the rulership over it could really be predicated only of one Personality. The question then arose, how to name and define that One? We might have expected that some one of the old gods would be erected into a truly monotheistic deity. But, perhaps because none of them seemed sufficiently superior to his fellows, perhaps for some other reason, this was not done. Instead, in a few late hymns of the Rig Veda we find various tentative efforts to establish a new deity in this supreme position. Different names are given to him: "the Lord of Creatures" (Prajāpati), "the All-maker" (Viśvakarman), and the like. As these names show, the new figure is rather abstract, and no longer ritualistic. Yet it is still personal. It is a *God* who creates, supports, and rules the world; a kind of Yahweh or Allah; not an impersonal First Cause. It is an attempt at monotheism, not yet monism.

These starts toward monotheism remained abortive, in the sense that they did not, at least directly, result in the establishment of a monotheistic religion comparable to that of the Hebrew people. Some centuries were to pass before such religions gained any strong foothold in India; and tenuous. The later religions owe their strength largely to other elements of more popular origin. Yet sporadic and more or less tentative suggestions of the sort continued to be made.

More striking, and more significant for the later development of Hindu philosophy, is a movement towards *monism* which appears, along with the monotheistic movement, even in the Rig Veda itself, though only tentatively and very rarely. One or two Rig-Vedic hymns attempt to formulate the One in strictly impersonal, nontheistic terms. Among these I must mention the one hundred and twenty-ninth hymn of the tenth book of the Rig Veda, which to my mind is a very remarkable production, considering its time and place. This "hymn" (for so we can hardly help calling it, since it is found in the "hymnbook" of the Rig Veda) also seeks to explain the universe as evolving out of One; but its One is no longer a god. It knows no Yahweh or Allah, any more than the ritualistic Indra or

Varuṇa. It definitely brushes aside all gods, but indeed denying their existence, but declaring that they are all of late and secondary origin; they know nothing of the beginnings of things. The First Principle of this hymn is "That One" (*tad ekam*). It is of neuter gender, as it were, lest some theologian should get hold of it and insist on falling down and worshiping it. It is not only impersonal and nontheistic, but absolutely uncharacterizable and indescribable, without qualities or attributes, even negative ones. It was "neither existent nor nonexistent." To seek to know it is hopeless; in the last two verses of the hymn (there are only seven in all) the author relapses into a negative style of expression which remains characteristic of Hindu higher thought in certain moods. While the later Upaniṣads often try to describe the One all-inclusively, by saying that it is *everything,* that it contains all possible and conceivable characteristics; still in some of their deepest moments they too prefer the negative statement *neti, neti*[1]—"No, no." To apply to it any description is to limit and bound that which is limitless and boundless. It cannot be described; it cannot be known.

But the ancient Hindu thinkers could never resign themselves to this negation. Even if they sometimes recognized that they could not, in the nature of things, know the Unknowable, still their restless speculation kept returning to the struggle again and again, from ever varied points of attack. In the Rig Veda itself, in one of its latest hymns (10.90), appears the first trace of a strain of monistic thought which is of the greatest importance for later Hindu philosophy: the universe is treated as parallel in nature to the human personality. The First Principle in this hymn is called Puruṣa—that is, "Man" or "Person." From the several parts of this cosmic Person are derived, by a still rather crude process of evolution, all existing things. The significance of this lies in its anticipation of the Upaniṣadic view of the identity of the human soul (later called *ātman,* literally "self," as a rule) with the universal principle.

Other, later Vedic texts, especially the Atharva Veda, also contain speculative materials. They are extremely varied in character; they testify to the restlessness and tentativeness which we have seen as a characteristic of all early Hindu thought. At times they seem monotheistic in tendency. The "Lord of Creatures," Prajāpati, of the Rig Veda, appears again and again, as a kind of demiurge; and other names are invented for the same or a similar figure, such as the "Establisher," Dhātar; or the "Arranger," Vidhātar; or "He that is in

[1] Bṛhad Āraṇyaka Upaniṣad 3.9.26, and in other places.

the Highest," Parameṣṭhin. But never does such a figure attain anything like the definite dignity which we associate with a genuine monotheistic deity. And more often the interest centers around less personal, more abstract entities, either physical or metaphysical, or more or less both at once. The sun, especially under the mystic name of Rohita, "The Ruddy One," enjoys a momentary glory in several Atharva-Vedic charms, which invest him with the functions of a cosmic principle. Or the world is developed out of water; we are reminded of Thales, the first of the Greek philosophers. The wind, regarded as the most subtle of physical elements and as the "life-breath" (prāṇa) of the universe, plays at times a like role, and by being compared with man's life-breath it contributes to the development of the cosmic "Person" (Puruṣa) of the Rig Veda into the later Ātman or Soul (of man) as the Supreme One. The word *ātman* itself seems actually to be used in this way in one or two late verses of the Atharva Veda.[2] The power of Time (*kāla*), or of Desire (*kāma*)—a sort of cosmic Will, reminding us of Schopenhauer—is elsewhere treated as the force behind the evolution of the universe. Or, still more abstractly, the world-all is derived from a hardly defined "Support"—that is, a "Fundamental Principle" (*skambha*)—on which everything rests. These and other shadowy figures flit across the stage of later Vedic speculation. Individually, few of them have enough definiteness or importance to merit much attention. But in the mass they are of the greatest value for one who would follow the development of Hindu speculation as a whole.

The real underlying motive and rationale of all this "monism," this seeking for a single principle in the universe, cannot be understood without reference to the principle of *identification* as it appears in early Vedic texts; most clearly in the Brāhmaṇas. A very striking feature of these works is their passion for identification of one thing with another, on the slenderest possible basis; indeed, often on no basis at all that we can discover. The purpose was strictly practical; more specifically, magical. It was to get results by setting cosmic forces in motion. To this end a cosmic force was said to "be" this or that other thing, which other thing we can control. "By grasping or controlling one of the two identified entities, the possessor of the mystic knowledge as to their identity has power over the other, which is in fact no other"[3] but really the same. For instance, "the cow is breath." I control a cow; therefore I control breath, my own

[2] 10.8.43,44.

[3] H. Oldenberg, *Vorwissenschaftliche Wissenschaft* (Göttingen, 1919), p. 110.

life-breath, or someone else's. That is the only reason for the fantastic identification. We want to control, let us say, the breath of life, in ourselves or someone else (perhaps an enemy): so we earnestly and insistently identify it with something that we *can* control, and the trick is turned. It required only a slight extension of this to arrive at the notion that if we can only "know" the one principle of the whole universe, the one which is to be *identified* with "all," with every thing that is, we shall then control all, and be able to deal with the universe as we please.[4] So all Vedic speculation is eminently practical. As we said above, metaphysical truth *per se* and for its own sake is not its object. Earnest and often profound though these thinkers are, they never lose sight for long of their practical aim, which is to control, by virtue of their superior knowledge, the cosmic forces which they study. That is why so many of their speculations are imbedded in the Atharva Veda, a book of magic spells, which to our minds would seem the most inappropriate place possible.

It might seem to follow from this that the speculative activity of this period belonged to the popular sphere represented by the religion of the Atharva Veda, more than to the ritualistic cult that was the heir of the Rig Veda. But I think there is evidence to the contrary. However appropriate to the spirit of the popular religion it seemed in some respects, this activity was carried on mainly by the priests of the hieratic ritual. And this fact, which for various reasons seems to me indubitable, finds a striking concrete expression in a philosophic term developed in this period which deserves special consideration.

Among all the varied formulations of the First and Supreme Principle, none recurs more constantly throughout the later Vedic texts than the *brahman*. The oldest meaning of this word seems to be "holy knowledge," "sacred utterance," or (what to primitive man is the same thing) its concrete expression, "hymn" or "incantation." It is applied both to the ritual hymns of the Rig Veda and to the magic charms of the Atharva Veda. Any holy, mystic utterance is *brahman*. This is the regular, if not the exclusive, meaning which the word has in the Rig Veda. But from the point of view of those times, this definition implies far more than it would suggest to our minds. The spoken word had a mysterious, supernatural power; it contained within itself the essence of the thing denoted. To "know the *name*" of anything was to control the thing. The *word* means

[4] See my article, "The Upaniṣads, what do they seek and why?" *Journal of the American Oriental Society,* Vol. 49, pp. 97 ff.

wisdom, knowledge; and knowledge, as we have seen, was (magic) power. So *brahman,* the "holy word," soon came to mean the mystic power inherent in the holy word.

But to the later Vedic ritualists, this holy word was the direct expression and embodiment of the ritual religion, and as such a cosmic power of the first magnitude. The ritual religion, and hence its verbal expression, the *brahman,* was omnipotent; it was "all." All human desires and aspirations were accessible to him who mastered it. All other cosmic forces, even the greatest of natural and supernatural powers, were dependent upon it. The gods themselves, originally the beneficiaries of the cult, became its helpless mechanical agents, or were left out of account altogether as useless middlemen. The cult was the direct controlling force of the universe. And the *brahman* was the spirit, the expression, of the cult; nay, it *was* the cult, mystically speaking, because the word and the thing were one; he who knew the word, knew and controlled the thing. Therefore, he who knew the *brahman* knew and controlled the whole universe. It is no wonder, then, that in the later Vedic texts (not yet in the Rig Veda) we find the *brahman* frequently mentioned as the primal principle[5] and as the ruling and guiding spirit of the universe. It is a thoroughly ritualistic notion, inconceivable except as an outgrowth of the theories of the ritualistic cult, but very simple and, as it were, self-evident from the point of view of the ritualists. The overwhelming prominence and importance of the *brahman* in later Vedic speculation seems, therefore, a striking proof of the fact that this speculation was at least in large part a product of ritualistic, priestly circles.

Not content with attempts to identify the One, the Vedic thinkers also try to define His, or Its, relation to the empiric world. Here again their suggestions are many and varied. Often the One is a sort of demiurge, a Creator, Father, First Cause. Such theistic expressions may be used for impersonal monistic names for the One as well as of more personal, quasi-monotheistic ones. The One is compared to a carpenter or a smith; he joins or smelts the world into being. Or his act is like an act of generation; he begets all beings. Still more interestingly, his creative activity is compared to a sacrifice, a ritual performance, or to prayer, or religious fervor (*dhī, tapas*). This obviously ritualistic imagery appears even in the Rig Veda itself, in several of its philosophic hymns. In the Puruṣa hymn, already re-

[5] "There is nothing more ancient or higher than this *brahman,*" Śatapatha Brāhmaṇa, 10.3.5.11.

ferred to, the universe is derived from the sacrifice of the cosmic Person, the Puruṣa; the figure is of the dismemberment of a sacrificial animal; from each of the members of the cosmic Puruṣa evolved a part of the existing world. The performers of this cosmogonic sacrifice are "the gods,"—inconsistently, of course, for the gods have already been declared to be secondary to the Puruṣa, who transcends all existing things. In later Vedic times we repeatedly meet with such ritualistic expressions. They confirm our feeling that we are dealing with priests.

We see from what has just been said of the Puruṣa hymn that the One—here the Puruṣa, the cosmic "Person" or "man"—may be regarded as the material source (*causa materialis*) as well as the creator (*causa efficiens*) of the world. All evolves out of it, or is a part of it; but frequently, as in the Puruṣa hymn, it is *more* than all empiric existence; it transcends all things, which form, or derive from, but a part of it. Again, it is often spoken of as the ruler, controller, or lord of all. Or, it is the foundation, fundament, upon which all is based, which supports all. Still more significant are passages which speak of the One as subtly pervading all, as air or ether or space (ākāśa) pervades the physical universe, and animating all, as the breath of life (prāṇa) is regarded as both pervading and animating the human body.

Such expressions as this last lead to a modification, with mitigation of the crudity, of the above-noted parallelism between man, the microcosm, and the universe, the macrocosm, which, as we have seen, dates from late Rig-Vedic times. In the Puruṣa hymn of the Rig Veda we find a crude evolution of various parts of the physical universe from the parts of the physical body of the cosmic "Man." But in the later Vedic texts the feeling grows that man's nature is not accounted for by dissecting his physical body—and, correspondingly, that there must be something more in the universe than the sum total of its physical elements. What is that "something more" in man? Is it the "life-breath" or "life-breaths" (prāṇa), which seem to be in and through various parts of the human body and to be the principle of man's life (since they leave the body at death)? So many Vedic thinkers believed. What, then, is the corresponding "life-breath" of the universe? Obviously the wind, say some. Others think of it as the ākāśa, "ether," or "space." But even these presently seem too physical, too material. On the human side, too, it begins to be evident that the "life-breath"—like its cosmic counterpart, the wind—is in reality physical. Surely the essential Man must be something else. What then? Flittingly, here and there, it is suggested that it may be man's "desire" or "will" (*kāma*), or his "mind" (*manas*), or something else of a more or less "psychological" nature. But already in the Atharva Veda, and with increasing frequency later, we find as an expression for the real, essential part of Man the word *ātman* used. *Ātman* means simply "self"; it is used familiarly as a reflexive pronoun, like the German *sich*. One could hardly get a more abstract term for that which is left when everything unessential is deducted from man, and which is at the same time to be considered the principle of his life, the living soul that pervades his being. And, carrying on the parallelism, we presently find mention of the *ātman,* self or soul, of the universe. The texts do not content themselves with that; they continue to speculate as to what that "soul" of the universe is. But these speculations tend to become more and more remote from purely physical elements. Increasing partiality is shown for such metaphysical expressions as "the existent," or "that which is" (*sat*),[6] or again "the nonexistent" (*asat*); in the Rig-Vedic hymn 10.129 we were told that in the beginning there was "neither existent nor nonexistent," but later we find both "the existent" and "the nonexistent" used as expressions for the first principle. But perhaps the favorite formula in later Vedic times for the soul of the universe is the originally ritualistic one of the *brahman*.

If we remember the Brāhmaṇa principle of identification by mystic knowledge for purposes of magical control, set forth above, we shall now be able to understand the standard answer given in the Upaniṣads to the question, "With what shall we identify the one thing, by knowing which all is known?" That answer is: "With the soul, the *ātman,* of man." Obviously; for whether it be called *Brahman,* or the existent, or what-not, the One is naturally the essential self or "soul," *ātman,* of the universe. If it is *ātman,* and my soul, my real self, is also *ātman,* then is not the mystic identification ready-made? By "knowing" the one, I may "know"—*and control*—the other. And surely there is nothing which I control more obviously and perfectly than my own "self." If now I "know" that the Brahman, which is the *ātman* of the universe, is my own *ātman,* then not only do I control the fundamental principle of the universe, be-

[6] Compare the Greek *τὸ ὄν* or *τὸ ὄντως ὄν*, "that which (really) is," and, for a less exact parallel, the Kantian *Ding an sich*. But the "existent," the "being," that which (really) is, whether in man or in the universe, was probably not so abstract or metaphysical as we feel the corresponding Western phrases. The Sanskrit word must be understood from the magical standpoint which I have described.

cause knowledge is magic power; but even more than that, I *am* the fundamental principle of the universe, by mystic identification. For this double reason, there is nothing beyond my grasp. Thus the knowledge of the One which is All, and its identification with the human soul, is a short cut to the satisfaction of all desires, the freedom from all fear and danger and sorrow.

# 7

# PREHISTORY OF THE GOD OF THE BHAGAVAD GĪTĀ


## Franklin Edgerton


The vast majority of Hindus are divided between the *vaiṣṇava* and *śaiva* sects, worshipers of *Viṣṇu* and *Śiva,* respectively. Brahmā, the titular head of the Hindu triad, is acknowledged, paid a scant homage, but counts with no real following.

The importance of the Gītā in India is that it provides its Hindu adherents with the kind of personal, benevolent, tangibly recognizable, and gracious divinity whom they can understand and who they feel can understand them: a god, in essence, who takes upon himself the main burden of the personal salvation of his devotees. A deity not unlike the Christian Saviour who gives of himself that man may not perish for all eternity.

We must face the fact that, by and large, whatever the religion, the requirements—indeed the demands—of the majority of adherents cannot and never have been satisfied by the theology, by the philosophically subtle speculative system, on which rests the religion in which we pretend to believe. If, as Christians, each of us were expected to be a Thomas Aquinas or a Paul Tillich, one wonders what would be the fate of Christianity. While a religion to be worthy of the name does require its Thomas Aquinases and its Paul Tillichs, its anonymous Upaniṣadic authors, its Buddhas and Mahāvīras, the majority of us demand and seldom rise above the level of religious "bread and circuses." Above all, we seem incapable of attaining by our own efforts the goal or goals that each religion sets for its adherents; there is everywhere the tacit—more frequently, explicit—admission that we are too weak (too human?) to look after our own individual spiritual welfare, to attain our religious objectives unaided. One might say we all want to have our religious cake and eat it, too.

From Franklin Edgerton, *The Bhagavad Gītā,* Harvard Oriental Series. Vol. 30 (1946). Copyright 1944 by The President and Fellows of Harvard College. Reprinted by permission of Harvard University Press.

In India the system expounded in the Upaniṣads, in the primitive Buddhism of Gautama the Buddha, and in the Jainism of Mahāvīra could never have, in their pure form, become popular religions. They were, as Edgerton says, "too speculative, too abstract" to have any popular appeal; they do not offer a helping hand, nor is there enough of bread and circuses in them. These early systems placed the burden of the attainment of the prescribed ends squarely upon the shoulders of the individual. Individual release, the attainment of *nirvāṇa,* was purely an individual matter; there was no one to whom the seeker after salvation could turn for assistance or comfort. There was, in short, no one to whom he could pray and onto whose broader shoulders he could shift the main burden of attaining release from *saṃsāra.* Something clearly had to be done if a popular base to these systems was to be developed, thus enabling them to survive. And something was indeed done.

Of the three systems of Jainism, Buddhism, and Hinduism, only the first never made an attempt to relax its requirements in order to attract popular support. While Jainism has known its moments of glory as the result of occasional royal patronage, it has always remained a rather exacting and austere system in which the individual is completely on his own when it comes to seeking release. It never spread beyond India and today numbers only a few million adherents. One should not conclude from this that Jains are somehow free of the bread-and-circuses complex. Jains participate in some of the Hindu rites, follow certain Hindu customs and employ Brahmins for certain purposes; such a situation, with the Jains having something of both worlds, may have precluded the development of Jainism in the direction of a popular cult.

Primitive Buddhism (as the religion which we assume was propounded by the Buddha is often called) was—like Jainism and Upaniṣadic Hinduism—austere, abstract, and demanding. Salvation, the attainment of *nirvāṇa,* was again a strictly personal, individual matter. Unlike Jainism, however, Buddhism developed popular tendencies—notably the Mahāyāna—with its deified Buddhas, including a Buddha of the future, and its benevolent, compassionate Bodhisattvas. The latter are there in order to relieve the individual of a considerable portion of the burden of attaining *nirvāṇa.* No doubt in large measure due to this popularization which tended to make postprimitive Buddhism hardly distinguishable from the popular Hinduism that was developing alongside it at that time, Buddhism all but disappeared from India. Having gone east and north to become one of the world's major religions, covering the Far East and Southeast Asia, Buddhism is practically unknown in the land of its birth.

Because of the royal patronage that Buddhism enjoyed—beginning with the Mauryas and especially under the Great Buddhist Emperor Aśoka—and because of its increasing similarity with Hinduism, one might legitimately wonder why it should have succumbed to Hinduism. Why, in sort, is India predominantly Hindu rather than Buddhist? The question smacks of one of those "contrary to fact" propositions so dear to older grammarians. Yet may not the answer lie in the very words "orthodox" and "heterodox"? It is not unlikely that Hinduism survived where Buddhism succumbed because it appealed to the conservative element in all men, accepting ties with the past that Buddhism more or less categorically rejected, providing thus something of continuity, some sense of identification with the past.

Hinduism's answer to the cry for bread and circuses in religion is perhaps best expressed in the Bhagavad Gītā. While not denying the validity of the ways of austerity and of altruism, of asceticism and of selfless action toward the attainment of *mokṣa,* the Gītā—in the person of Viṣnu-Kṛṣṇa, the personal, compassionate divinity—effectively removes the "gates of heaven" from their hinges. By offering the way of *bhakti,* personal devotion to the deity (Viṣṇu-Kṛṣṇa), as a means of attaining release from *saṃsāra,* the Gītā extends hope to the followers of the *ordinary* norm. Now all men—the ascetic, the selfless altruist, the "normal," and the "average"—can attain their religious goal.

It could hardly be expected that the popular interest would be gripped by Upaniṣadic thought. It was too speculative, too abstract, to appeal to any but a small proportion of the population. The great mass of mankind demanded, as always, a personal, quasi-human god or gods to worship; it could not be satisfied by mystic contemplation of a nameless Soul, even if it be the Soul of the universe. Some more acceptable outlet for the religious feeling of the people had to be provided; and there is good reason to believe that it was provided. Unfortunately, the evidence about it is mostly indirect and secondary. We can judge of it, for the most part, only from its traces in such later works as the Bhagavad Gītā, which clearly presuppose a considerable development of popular religion, distinct from the higher thought of the Upaniṣads but contemporary therewith. In the Gītā these two streams are blended. We have no records that show us the popular beliefs of that period in a pure form.

For this reason, it is scarcely possible to attempt any extensive reconstruction of those popular beliefs. The principal thing to be said about them is that they were certainly theistic, and presumably tended towards a monotheism, of a more or less qualified sort. That is, presumably various local or tribal deities were worshipped in different parts of India, each occupying a position somewhat similar to that of Yahweh among the Jews—each being regarded as the chief or perhaps the sole god of his people or tribe, though the existence of the gods of other tribes was not denied. These local deities were, we may assume, of very different types and origins. Sometimes they may have been old gods of aboriginal, non-Aryan tribes. Sometimes they seem to have been local heroes, deified after death.

Such a local deity must have been the Kṛṣṇa who appears as the Supreme Deity, the "Blessed One," in the Bhagavad Gītā. He was apparently a deified local chieftain, the head of the Vṛṣṇi clan. Indeed, he appears as such, in strictly human guise, in the greater part of the Mahābhārata. In the Gītā he is still both god and man; an incarnation of the Deity in human form. We know nothing of the process by which he attained divine honors, nor of his earlier history as a god, before the Bhagavad Gītā, which is probably the earliest work preserved to us in which he appears as such. In this work he has all the attributes of a full-fledged monotheistic deity, and at the same time, as we shall see, the attributes of the Upaniṣadic Absolute. In other words, the popular God is philosophized into a figure who can appeal to both the higher and the lower circles of the population. Therein lies the strength of Kṛṣṇaism in later India; it is many-sided enough to satisfy the religious requirements of almost any man, whatever his intellectual or social status may be.

The Upaniṣads themselves are not entirely free from quasi-Monotheistic touches, some of which may perhaps be interpreted as concessions to this same popular demand for a personal god. Especially interesting, and important for later Hinduism, is the personalization of the philosophic term Brahman, as a name for the Absolute, which appears even in some of the earliest Upaniṣads. The word *brahman* is primarily and originally neuter in gender, and remains so usually throughout the Upaniṣads and the Bhagavad Gītā; but occasionally it acquires a personality, as a sort of creating and ruling deity, and then it has masculine gender. It thus becomes the god Brahmā, familiar to later Hinduism as the nominal head of the Triad consisting of Brahmā the Creator, Viṣṇu the Preserver, and Śiva the Destroyer. This trinity appears only in comparatively late Upaniṣads, and no clear mention of it is found in the Bhagavad Gītā, altho the Gītā at least once refers to the masculine and personal Brahmā, "the Lord sitting on the lotus-seat." [1] But this grammatical trick was not

[1] xi. 15.

sufficient to satisfy the craving of the men of India. Even masculinized, Brahman-Brahmā remained too bloodless to attract many worshipers. Later Hinduism pays lip-homage to him, but reserves its real worship for his colleagues, Viṣṇu and Śiva.

Viṣṇu and Śiva, under various names and forms, are the real gods of later India. Śiva-worship, though certainly much older than the Bhagavad Gītā, hardly appears therein,[2] and may therefore be left out of consideration in this book. But we must say a few words about Viṣṇu, since he was identified with Kṛṣṇa, the Gītā's God, or regarded as incarnate in Him. This identification seems to me to appear clearly in the Gītā itself.[3]

Viṣṇu was one of the gods of the Rig Veda, and probably, like most of them, a nature-god. He seems to have been a personification of the sun. But the Rig Veda contains a number of sun-gods (perhaps originally belonging to different tribes, or else representing different aspects of the sun's power). Viṣṇu is one of the less prominent and less important ones. He is distinctly a minor figure in the Rig Veda. We hear that he measures the universe in three great strides, which refer figuratively to the sun's progress across the sky. The third stride lands him in "the highest footstep (or place; the word has both meanings) of Viṣṇu," which means the zenith. This is thought of as the highest point in the universe, and at times it is described as a kind of solar paradise, to which the spirits of the blessed dead may go. So in post-Rig-Vedic literature, we hear expressions of the desire for attaining "Viṣṇu's highest place." So, also, in this period, Viṣṇu is occasionally declared to be "the highest of the gods"; this is doubtless to be understood in a literal, physical sense, because Viṣṇu's abode is the "top of the world." In the same period, we find very frequently the statement that "Viṣṇu is the sacrifice." Why he should have been singled out for this honor, we cannot tell; there are other gods whose far greater prominence would seem to us to give them a better claim to be regarded as a personification of the ritual. But the frequency of the statement leaves no room for doubt that the priests of the "Middle Vedic" (Brāhmaṇa) period generally regarded Viṣṇu in this way. And since, as we have seen to them the "sacrifice" was

[2] Śiva, under various of his innumerable names is, however, mentioned (for example, x.23).

[3] A distinguished Hindu scholar, the late Sir R. G. Bhandarkar, thought that Kṛṣṇa was not yet identified with Viṣṇu in the Gītā, though he was soon afterwards. See his *Vaiṣṇavism, Śaivism and Minor Religious Systems,* page 13. But Kṛṣṇa is directly addressed as Viṣṇu in xi.24 and 30; and I do not believe that Viṣṇu can here mean "the sun."

the central power of the universe, we see that from their point of view no higher compliment was possible. Evidently Viṣṇu was acquiring a much more dignified position than he had in the Rig Veda.

The Upaniṣads add nothing to the history of Viṣṇu. They—that is, the older ones, those which antedate the Gītā—mention his name only three or four times, and quite in the style of the Middle-Vedic period. But suddenly, in the Gītā and other contemporary writings, we find Viṣṇu recognized as a supreme monotheistic deity, worshiped either under his own name, or in the form of various incarnations, the chief of which is Kṛṣṇa. This was at a time when the Vedic religion, as a whole, was nearly dead. Its gods no longer had a real hold on any class of the people. Their existence was not denied, but they were reduced to the rank of petty spirits. Even the once all-important sacrifices were largely falling into disuse. But if the ritual religion was perishing, the priestly class was not. By this time it was recognized as a definite and hereditary caste, the brahmanhood, which claimed the headship of human society. With this fact, probably, is to be connected the identification of the god or hero Kṛṣṇa, and other popular gods and heroes, with the old Vedic god Viṣṇu. Thus a sacerdotal tinge was given to the thriving monotheism which had such a hold on the mass of the people. Brahmanism stooped to conquer; it absorbed popular cults which it had not the strength to uproot. The simple and ancient device of identification of one god with another furnished the means to this end.

It remains something of a mystery to scholars why Viṣṇu, rather than some other Vedic deity, was selected for this purpose. Even after the development described in the last paragraph but one, Viṣṇu is by no means the most prominent god of the pantheon. Many steps in the long process have evidently disappeared from our sight. But probably his frequent identification with the sacrifice, and his growing eschatological importance as the ruler of a kind of paradise for the dead in his "highest place," have something to do with it.

We have, then, finally, a union of at least three strands in the monotheistic deity of the Bhagavad Gītā: a popular god-hero of a local tribe, an ancient Vedic deity belonging to the hieratic ritual religion, and the philosophic Absolute of the Upaniṣads. The blend is, as we shall see, by no means perfect. Especially the monistic, Upaniṣadic element is sometimes rather clearly distinguished from the theistic element or elements; the author of the Gītā himself underlines this distinction at times. But for the most part it is hard to disentangle one from the other.

# 8

# PRACTICAL MORALITY

## Franklin Edgerton

The following selection is quite self-explanatory; it is, as are the two preceding selections, based on the Bhagavad Gītā. The most I can do at this juncture is to give something of the *mise en scène,* alluded to in this selection, of that remarkable document.

The Gītā, while actually standing on its own as one of the most important documents of Hinduism (as distinct from the earlier Brahmanical or Vedic system), is actually but a part—interpolated no doubt—of the major epic of India, the Mahābhārata. This work tells of the mighty struggle of the Kauravas and the Pāṇḍavas for supremacy in the land: The one hundred Kaurava brothers, under the leadership of their father, the blind Dhṛtarāṣṭra, and their eldest brother, Duryodhana, are pitted against their cousins, the five Pāṇḍavas (the sons of Pāṇḍu, brother to Dhṛtarāṣṭra), led nominally by the eldest, Yudhiṣṭhira, but whose great hero (in the Gītā at any rate) is brother number three, Arjuna.

The Gītā opens magnificently: the two armies arrayed, ready to do battle, on the ancestral field of Kuru; pennons flapping in the breeze and horses pawing the ground impatiently. As the conch shells signal the beginning of the battle, and as the armies are about to hurl themselves upon each other, Arjuna has doubts about the bloody deeds he is on the verge of perpetrating—the slaying of his kinsman, teachers, friends—and he voices his doubts to his charioteer, none other than the lord Kṛṣṇa himself. Kṛṣṇa (Viṣṇu) then tells Arjuna why he must take part in the upcoming battle, why he has in reality no alternative but to do so (his *dharma,* his duty as a Kṣatriya). Kṛṣṇa then proceeds to expound the unique philosophy of the Bhagavad Gītā, including the essence of practical morality.

Franklin Edgerton, *The Bhagavad Gītā,* Harvard Oriental Series, Vol. 30 (1946). 

The Gītā's attitude toward practical morality is characteristic of most Hindu religions. In its relation to the ultimate goal of salvation, morality is only a secondary means. It alone is never sufficient to achieve that goal. But on the other hand it leads to ever better and higher existences, and helps to prepare for final success.

The importance of morality comes out most clearly on the negative side. Immorality is clearly regarded as a serious, indeed usually a fatal, hindrance. To be sure we are told that "if even a very wicked man worships Me with single devotion, he is to be regarded as righteous after all; for he has the right resolution"; and again that "even if thou shouldst be the worst sinner of all sinners, thou shalt cross over all (the 'sea' of) evil merely by the boat of knowledge." These passages suggest a sort of magic absolution from sin by devotion to God, or to knowledge, as the case may be. It might be inferred from them that it makes little or no difference what a man may do, so long as he succeeds in possessing himself of the key to salvation. This is, however, probably not a fair inference from the Gītā's words. In the first place we must remember that the Gītā is poetic in its language and not infrequently emphasizes its ideas by a certain overstatement. To drive home the importance of "devotion" or "knowledge" it attributes to each of them in turn the power to absolve from the most heinous sins. Secondly, the Gītā undoubtedly means to imply a reformation and repentance on the part of the sinner as a prerequisite, or at least concomitant, to the attainment of "devotion" or "knowledge." We are, indeed, told elsewhere in definite terms that wicked men cannot, in the nature of things, possess true devotion or knowledge either. "Wicked and deluded evil-doers do not resort to Me; their intelligence is taken away by (My) illusion (*māyā*), and they remain in the 'demoniac' condition." (We shall see what is meant by the "demoniac" condition in the next paragraph.) In another passage "knowledge" is defined at length in distinctly ethical terms; that is, he who is wise is necessarily also righteous, as Socrates said. Knowledge includes "absence of pride and deceit, harmlessness, patience, uprightness, devotion to one's teacher, purity, firmness, self-control, aversion to the objects of sense, unselfishness," and so forth; "indifference" and "devotion to God" are also included. Again a description of the qualities of the perfected man, who is fit for union with Brahman, includes abstention from lust and hatred and from such vices as selfishness, violence, pride, desire, and anger.

The sixteenth chapter of the Gītā is wholly devoted to a sort of practical moral code. It tells us that there are two kinds of "nature" or "condition" or "estate" of man, the "divine" and the "demoniac";

that is, the good and the bad, the sheep and the goats. The good estate tends towards emancipation, the bad towards continued bondage in existence. That is, more explicitly, men who are bad or "demoniac" by nature are reborn again and again; they fail to reach God, and their fate is wretched, while the good come finally to salvation. The good are characterized by "fearlessness, purification of being, steadfastness in the discipline of knowledge (or knowledge and disciplined activity), generosity, self-control, sacrifice, (religious) study, austerities, and uprightness; harmlessness, truth, freedom from anger, abandonment (or generosity), serenity, freedom from malice, compassion to all creatures, uncovetousness, gentleness, modesty, no fickleness; majesty, patience, fortitude, purity, nonviolence, freedom from pride." The characteristics of the wicked are described and illustrated at much greater length. In general they are, of course, the opposites of the qualities just mentioned. But emphasis is laid on the ignorance of the wicked, on their materialistic and atheistic philosophy, on their overweening pride and stupid self-confidence. "Resorting to egotism, violence, arrogance, lust, and wrath, they hate Me in their own bodies and those of others, these envious men"; that is, by their misdeeds they wrong God, who is in themselves and in other men. All their vices are finally traced to three primary vices, desire or lust, wrath, and greed, "a threefold gate to hell, destroying the soul." He who is subject to them cannot hope for perfection or bliss. In another passage desire or lust and wrath are referred to as the twin causes of all vice. This seems indeed sufficient, since avarice or greed is only a specialized form of desire or lust. "Desire and loathing" is the formula in other places. And since "loathing" is merely negative desire, while "wrath" or "passion" is only a pragmatic manifestation or result of desire, whether positive or negative, we find that in the last analysis "desire" is the root of all evil.

One positive feature of the Gītā's morality deserves special mention. The metaphysical doctrine that the one universal Soul is in all creatures furnishes an admirable basis for a very lofty type of morality. Since one's own Self or Soul is really identical with the Self or Soul of all other creatures, therefore one who injures others injures himself. "For beholding the same Lord (the universal Soul) residing in all beings, a man does not harm himself (his own self in others) by himself; so he goes to the final goal." Thus one of the most striking and emphatic of the ethical doctrines of the Gītā is substantially that of the Golden Rule. Man must treat all creatures alike, from the highest to the lowest—namely, like himself. The perfected man "delights in the welfare of all beings." This principle is usually regarded as perhaps the highest formulation of practical ethics that any religion has attained. It is interesting to see how naturally and simply it follows from one of the most fundamental tenets of the Gītā's philosophy.

A genuine application of this moral principle would seem almost inevitably to include avoidance of any violent injury to living beings. And, as is well known, most Hindu sects have in fact applied it in this way, at least in theory, and to a considerable extent in practice. "Nonviolence" or "harmlessness" (*ahiṃsā*) has generally been accepted as a cardinal virtue. It finds expression, for instance, in the vegetarian diet which so many Hindus have always favored, and in the policy of pacifism and "passive resistance" which, while never adopted universally, has probably had more followers at every period in India than in most other lands.

The Gītā's morality on this point is somewhat disappointing. It does indeed include "harmlessness" or "nonviolence" (*ahiṃsā*) in several of its lists of virtues. But it never singles it out for special emphasis. It seems to be content to let it lie buried in such more or less formal moral catalogs. One gets the impression that it was too prominent and well-recognized a virtue to be ignored; so some lip-homage is paid to it. But it is never definitely and sharply applied in such a form as "Thou shalt not kill." The Gītā contrasts strikingly in this respect with some other Hindu sects, such as the Buddhists and (still more) the Jains. It seems a little strange, at first sight, to find any Hindu religious text treating the doctrine of nonviolence in so stepmotherly a fashion. But of course the reason is quite evident. The Gītā is hampered by the fact that it is supposed to justify Arjuna's participation in war. This dramatic situation is alluded to repeatedly, and the author seems to have it in the back of his head a large part of the time. To be sure, many of his doctrines are inconsistent enough with such a purpose, as we have abundantly seen. And we must not forget, either, that "noninjury" is clearly implied in the Gītā's teachings on the subject of unselfishness and doing good to others. That is, to carry out these teachings in any real sense would necessarily involve doing no harm to living creatures. But to lay a frank and full emphasis upon this principle, to follow it out explicitly to its logical conclusion, would mean to run so glaringly counter to the professed aim of the piece, that it is not strange that the author avoids doing so. Even his catholicity seems to have shrunk from such an inconsistency as that. We can hardly help feeling, however, that he lost a golden opportunity thereby.

# 9

# THE BACKGROUND OF JAINISM AND BUDDHISM

The following three selections deal with the two so-called heterodox systems that arose at the same time as Hinduism in the Epic Period. The first deals with the subject generally; the next two, specifically. I would only ask the reader to bear in mind that the terms "orthodox" and "heterodox" must be taken with some caution. While we can—from the standpoint of continuity with elements of the Aryan tradition, the acceptance of certain institutions—speak of Hinduism as "orthodox" and of Jainism and Buddhism as "heterodox," the three are almost equally radical departures from the Vedic or Brahmanical past; the three systems are Indian, and thus more substantially alike than any one of them, not excluding Hinduism, is like the system of the preceding era.

The first of the selections "The Background of Jainism and Buddhism," might also serve to point up the extent of the speculation of the period that gave us the three religious systems here treated. The fact is that these three survived, while many others, the products of the same period and of the same forces, did not.

Between the seventh and the fifth centuries B.C. the intellectual life of India was in ferment. It has been pointed out many times that this period was a turning point in the intellectual and spiritual development of the whole world, for it saw the earlier philosophers of Greece, the great Hebrew prophets, Confucius in China, and probably Zarathustra in Persia. In India this crucial period in the world's history was marked on the one hand by the teaching of the Upanishadic sages, who admitted the inspiration of the Vedas and the relative value of Vedic sacrifices, and on the other hand by the appearance of teachers who were less orthodox than they, and who rejected the Vedas entirely. It was at this time that Jainism and Buddhism arose, the most successful of a large number of heterodox systems, each based on a distinctive set of doctrines and each laying down distinctive rules of conduct for winning salvation.

The social background of this great development of heterodoxy cannot be traced as clearly as we would wish from the traditions of Jainism and Buddhism, which have to some extent been worked over by editors of later centuries. But it would appear that heterodoxy flourished most strongly in what is now the state of Bihar and the eastern part of Uttar Pradesh. Here the arrival of Aryan civilization and brahmanical religion seems to have been comparatively recent at the time. The people were probably little affected by the Aryan class system, and the influence of the brāhman was by no means complete. Quite as much attention was devoted to local chthonic gods such as yakshas and nāgas, worshipped at sacred mounds and groves (chaityas), as to the deities of the Aryan pantheon. Cities had arisen, where a class of well-to-do merchants lived in comparative opulence, while the free peasants who made up the majority of the population enjoyed, as far as can be gathered, a somewhat higher standard of living than they do today, when pressure of population and exhaustion of the soil have so gravely impoverished them.

The old tribal structure was disintegrating, and a number of small regional kingdoms had appeared, together with political units of a somewhat different type, which preserved more of the tribal structure, and are generally referred to as "republics" for want of a better word. Most of these republics were of little importance politically, and were dependent on the largest of the kingdoms, Kosala, which controlled most of the eastern part of modern Uttar Pradesh; one such was that of the Shākyas, in the Himalayan foothills, which might well have been forgotten entirely were it not for the fact that the founder of Buddhism was the son of one of its chiefs. The most important of these republics was that generally referred to as the Vajjian Confederacy, of which the largest element was the tribe of the Licchavis; this controlled much of Bihar north of the Ganges, and was apparently governed by a chief who derived his power from a larger assembly of tribesmen, and ruled with the aid of a small council of lesser chiefs. Much of Bihar south of the Ganges formed the kingdom of Magadha. King Bimbīsara, who ruled Magadha during most of the time in which the Buddha taught, seems to have had more initiative in political organization than his rivals, and managed his little state with more efficiency and closer centralized control than any other chief or king of his time. His son, Ajātasattu, who began to reign some seven years before the Buddha's death, embarked upon a policy of expansion. Magadha soon absorbed the Vajjis and Kosala, and her growth continued until, about two hundred years later, the great emperor Ashoka annexed Kalinga, and Pātaliputra (modern Patna) became the capital of the whole Indian subcontinent except the southern tip.

The development of organized states and the advance of material culture were accompanied by the rapid spread of new religious ideas which were soon to become fundamental to all Indian thought. It is remarkable that in the Vedas and the earlier Brāhmana literature the doctrine of transmigration[1] is nowhere clearly mentioned, and there is no good reason to believe that the Aryans of Vedic times accepted it. It first appears, in a rather primitive form, in the early Upanishads as a rare and new doctine, to be imparted as a great mystery by master-hermits to their more promising pupils. In the next stratum of India's religious literature, the Jain and Buddhist scriptures, the doctrine of transmigration is taken for granted, and has evidently become almost universal. With this belief in transmigration came a passionate desire for escape, for union with something which lay beyond the dreary cycle of birth and death and rebirth, for timeless being, in place of transitory and therefore unsatisfactory existence. The rapid spread of belief in transmigration throughout the whole of northern India is hard to account for; it may be that the humbler strata of society had believed in some form of transmigration from time immemorial, but only now did it begin to affect the upper classes. It is equally difficult to explain the growth of a sense of dissatisfaction with the world and of a desire to escape from it. Several reasons have been suggested to account for this great wave of pessimism, occurring as it did in an expanding society, and in a culture which was rapidly developing both intellectually and materially. It has been suggested that the change in outlook was due to the breakup of old tribes and their replacement by kingdoms wherein ethnic ties and the sense of security which they gave were lost or weakened, thus leading to a deep-seated psychological unease affecting all sections of the people. Another suggested cause of the

[1] We use this term, which is the most usual one, with reference to the general Indian doctrine of reincarnation and rebirth; but it must be remembered that it is misleading when applied to Buddhism, which maintains that no entity of any kind migrates from one body to another.

change in outlook is the revolt of the most intelligent people of the times against the sterile sacrificial cults of the brāhmans. No explanation is wholly satisfactory, and we must admit our virtual ignorance of the factors which led to this great change in the direction of religious thought which was to have such an effect on the life of India and the world.

Both the sages of the Upanishads and the heresiarchs of the unorthodox schools taught the way of knowledge, as opposed to the way or works. Their primary aim was to achieve salvation from the round of birth and death, and to lead others to achieve it. Most of them maintained that salvation could only be obtained after a long course of physical and mental discipline, often culminating in extreme asceticism, but this was chiefly of value as leading to the full realization of the fundamental truths of the universe, after which the seeker for salvation was emancipated from the cycle of transmigration and reached a state of timeless bliss in which his limited phenomenal personality disintegrated or was absorbed in pure being. The basic truths of the various schools differed widely.

In many passages of the Buddhist scriptures we read of six unorthodox teachers (often rather inaccurately referred to as "heretics"), each of whom was the leader of an important body of ascetics and lay followers. In one passage (*Dīgha Nikāya* 1.47 ff.) short paragraphs are quoted which purport to give the basic tenets of their systems. A glance at these will give some impression of the bewildering variety of doctrines which were canvassed by the ascetic groups of the time.

The first of the teachers mentioned, Pūrana Kassapa, was an antinomian, who believed that virtuous conduct had no effect on a man's karma:

> He who performs an act or causes an act to be performed, . . . he who destroys life, the thief, the housebreaker, the plunderer, . . . the adulterer and the liar . . . commit no sin. Even if with a razor-sharp discus a man were to reduce all the life on earth to a single heap of flesh he would commit no sin, neither would sin approach him. . . . From liberality, self-control, abstinence, and honesty is derived neither merit nor the approach of merit.

The second "heretic," Makkhali Gosāla, was the leader of the sect of Ājīvikas, which survived for some two thousand years after the death of its founder. He agreed with Pūrana that good deeds did not affect transmigration, which proceeded according to a rigid pattern, controlled by an all-powerful cosmic principle which he called *Niyati,* Fate.

> There is no deed performed either by oneself or by others [which can affect one's future births], no human action, no strength, no courage, no human endurance or human prowess [which can affect one's destiny in this life]. All beings, all that have breath, all that are born, all that have life, are without power, strength, or virtue, but are developed by destiny, chance, and nature. . . . There is no question of bringing unripe karma[2] to fruition, nor of exhausting karma already ripened, by virtuous conduct, by vows, by penance, or by chastity. That cannot be done. Samsāra[3] is measured as with a bushel, with its joy and sorrow and its appointed end. It can neither be lessened nor increased, nor is there any excess or deficiency of it. Just as a ball of thread will, when thrown, unwind to its full length, so fool and wise alike will take their course, and make an end of sorrow.

The third heterodox teacher, Ajita Kesakambala, was a materialist. The passage in which his views are given is one of the earliest expressions of complete unbelief in immaterial categories in the history of the world's thought:

> There is no [merit in] almsgiving, sacrifice, or offering, no result or ripening of good or evil deeds. There is no passing from this world to the next. . . . There is no after-life. . . . Man is formed of the four elements; when he dies earth returns to the aggregate of earth, water to water, fire to fire, and air to air, while the senses vanish into space. Four men with the bier take up the corpse; they gossip [about the dead man] as far as the burning ground, where his bones turn the color of a dove's wings, and his sacrifices end in ashes. They are fools who preach almsgiving, and those who maintain the existence of immaterial categories speak vain and lying nonsense. When the body dies, both fool and wise alike are cut off and perish. They do not survive after death.

[2] It is perhaps unnecessary to mention that karma is the effect of any action upon the agent, whether in this life or in a future one. Most Indian sects believed that karma operated as a sort of automatic moral sanction, ensuring that the evil-doer suffered and the righteous prospered; but Pūrana, Makkhali, and Pakudha appear to have disagreed with this view, while Ajita, the materialist, evidently denied the existence of karma altogether. The Jains, as we shall see, still look on karma as a sort of substance adhering to the soul, and it would appear that the "heretics" did likewise, although later Hinduism and Buddhism take a less materialistic view of it.

[3] The cycle of transmigration, the round of birth, death, and rebirth.

Pakudha Kacchāyana, the fourth of the six, was an atomist, a predecessor of the Hindu Vaisheshika school, putting forward his theories probably a century or more before Democritus in Greece developed a similar doctrine of eternal atoms:

> The seven elementary categories are neither made nor ordered, neither caused nor constructed; they are barren, as firm as mountains, as stable as pillars. They neither move nor develop; they do not injure one another, and one has no effect on the joy or the sorrow . . . of another. What are the seven? The bodies of earth, water, fire, air, joy and sorrow, with life as the seventh. . . . No man slays or causes to slay, hears or causes to hear, knows or causes to know. Even if a man cleave another's head with a sharp sword, he does not take life, for the sword-cut passes between the seven elements.[4]

The fifth teacher, Nigantha Nātaputta, was no other than Vardhamāna Mahāvīra, the leader of the sect of Jains, which survives to this day, and the teachings of which will be considered presently. The sixth and last, Sanjaya Belatthiputta, was, as far as can be gathered from the passage attributed to him, a sceptic, who denied the possibility of certain knowledge altogether:

> If you asked me, "Is there another world?" and if I believed that there was, I should tell you so. But that is not what I say. I do not say that it is so; I do not say that it is otherwise; I do not say that it is not so; nor do I say that it is not not so.

It must be emphasized that the salvation promised by these teachers, and by others like them, was not dependent on the mere acceptance of the doctrine on the word of the teacher, or on belief in it on a cool logical basis. To achieve release from transmigration it was necessary that the fundamental doctrine should be realized in the inmost being of the individual, and such a realization could only be achieved by the mystical and ascetic practices generally known in the West as yoga. Each group, even that of the materialists who followed Ajita, had its special system of meditation and mental or spiritual exercises, each its organized body of followers, usually ascetics, pledged to strive together for emancipation. Lay devotees and patrons were generally thought to be on the lowest rungs of the spiritual ladder, and there was little or no chance of full salvation outside the disciplined order.

[4] These doctrines were apparently taken up by the Ājīvikas, who in later times maintained a theory of seven elements, which was evidently derived from that of Pakudha.

# 10

# THE BASIC DOCTRINES OF JAINISM

Jainism is a system little known and less understood outside of India, yet in Indian religious and philosophical thought it is no less important than the better known Hinduism and Buddhism. Jainism is of interest to the Indologist and to the student of religion because of its frank materialism and its avowed atheism. (Primitive Buddhism is only inferentially atheistic.) Jainism's materialism and atheism are of the kind, moreover, that seem to make sense; one of the difficulties with Jain materialism, however, is the logical contradiction (in our own Western terms) implicit in the inexhaustability of material lives or *jīvas*.

On the more general level the Indologist, as implied in this selection, is forever beholden to the Jain monks for the careful preservation of hundreds of documents, Jain and non-Jain, secular and non-secular, that otherwise surely would have perished.

Originating at the same time and in the same region of India as Buddhism, Jainism has experienced its moments of triumph, periods when mighty kings supported it and the finest draftsmen in India worked on the embellishment of its temples. But it has never spread, like Buddhism, beyond the land of its origin to become one of the world's great religions; on the other hand, it has not disappeared from India as Buddhism has, but has survived to the present day, a small but significant element in the religious life of the subcontinent.

## THE ORIGIN AND DEVELOPMENT OF JAINISM

The figure to whom Jains look back as their great teacher, Vardhamāna Mahāvīra ("The Great Hero"), was a contemporary of the Buddha, often mentioned in the Buddhist scriptures under the name of Nigantha Nātaputta, "the naked ascetic of the clan of Jnātrikas." Mahāvīra is believed by the Jains to have been the twenty-fourth and last Tīrthankara ("Fordmaker") of the present period of cosmic decline. Pārshva, the twenty-third Tīrthankara, is said to have lived only two hundred and fifty years before Mahāvīra, and it would seem that in fact the latter teacher based his new community on existing groups of ascetics, some of whom looked back to the earlier preacher Pārshva. The legends told by the Jains about Mahāvīra are in many ways less attractive than those told by Buddhists about Buddha, and most of them are equally doubtful from the point of view of the historian, but the main outline of his life-story is probably true. Mahāvīra is said to have been the son of Siddhārtha, a chief of the warrior clan of the Jnātrikas, and his wife Trishalā, sister of Chetaka, chief of the larger kindred tribe of the Licchavis; both tribes dwelled around the important city of Vaishāli, in what is now North Bihar. Thus, like the Buddha, Mahāvīra was a scion of the tribal "republican" peoples of India. He is said to have left his home at the age of thirty in order to seek salvation and to have wandered for twelve years far and wide in the Ganges valley, until, at the age of forty-two, he found full enlightenment, and became a "completed soul" (kevalin) and a "conqueror" (jina). From a derivative form of the second title, the Jains take their name. Mahāvīra taught his doctrines for some thirty years, founding a disciplined order of naked monks and gaining the support of many layfolk. He died at the age of seventy-two at Pāvām, a village not far from Patna, which is still visited by thousands of Jains annually and is one of their most sacred places of pilgrimage. Most authorities believe that the date of his death was 468 B.C., although Jains themselves place it some sixty years earlier.

Probably for a century or so after Mahāvīra's death, the Jains were comparatively unimportant, because both the Jain and the Buddhist scriptures, though not wholly ignoring the existence of the other sect, look on the sect of the Ājīvikas as the chief rival of their respective faiths. Jainism, like Buddhism, began to flourish in the days of the Mauryas. A very strong Jain tradition maintains that the first Maurya emperor, Chandragupta (circa 317-293 B.C.), was a patron of Jainism and ultimately became a Jain monk. It is to this period that the great schism in Jainism is attributed by tradition. Between the death of Mahāvīra and this time, the order had been led by a series of pontiffs called *Gaṇadharas* ("Supporters of the Communities"). Bhadrabāhu, the eleventh *Gaṇadhara,* foresaw that a great famine would soon occur in northern India, and so, with a great following of naked monks, among whom was the ex-emperor Chandragupta, he departed for the Deccan, leaving behind many monks who refused to follow him, under the leadership of another teacher, Sthūlabhadra. When the famine was over, Bhadrabāhu and many of the exiles returned to find that those who had remained in the north had adopted many dubious practices as a result of the distress and confusion of the famine, the most censurable of which was the wearing of white robes.

This, however, was not the only misfortune resulting from the famine. Bhadrabāhu was the only person who knew perfectly the unwritten sacred texts of Jainism. In order to conserve them, Sthūlabhadra called a council of monks at Pātaliputra, but Bhadrabāhu was not present; horrified at the corruption of the Order he had departed for Nepal to end his days in solitary fasting and penance. So the original canon of Jainism was reconstructed as well as possible from the defective memory of Sthūlabhadra and other leading monks in the form of the eleven *Limbs* (Aṅga). Thus, according to tradition, Jainism was divided into two great sections, though in fact the division may have existed in germ in the days of Mahāvīra himself and did not become final until about two centuries later. On the one hand were the *Digambaras,* the "Space-Clad," who insisted on the total nudity of their monks and who did not admit the full authenticity of the eleven *Limbs,* and on the other the *Shvetāmbaras,* or "White-Clad," whose monks wore white robes and who accepted the *Limbs.* Today the Digambaras are to be found chiefly in the Deccan, especially in Mysore, while the Shvetāmbaras, who are much in the majority, dwell chiefly in Gujarat and Rajasthan. Though the teachers of one group would in the past often write and speak very acrimoniously about the practices of the other, there has never been any fundamental difference in doctrine. There was no development in Jainism at all comparable to that which produced Mahāyāna Buddhism from Theravāda. All Jains, whatever their sect, maintain the same fundamental teachings, which have probably been little altered since the time of Bhadrabāhu. Though there have been superficial compromises with Hinduism, Jainism remains what it was over two thousand years ago.

There is no doubt that Jain monks did much to spread northern culture in the Deccan and the Tamil land, and in the early medieval period, until the eleventh century, many important south Indian kings gave Jainism their support. But the great wave of devotional theism which arose in south India almost overwhelmed it, and it never again became a major force in the religious life of the peninsula. In the west, too, after a period of triumph in the twelfth century, when King Kumārapāla of Gujarat became an earnest Jain, the religion declined. But its layfolk, unlike those of Buddhism, were bound to their faith by carefully regulated observances and the pastoral care of the monks. Solidly knit communities of well-to-do merchants forming their own castes, the Jains resisted both the violent attacks of the Muslims and the constant peaceful pressure of the brāhmins; where Buddhism perished, Jainism survived.

Indeed in recent centuries Jainism has shown signs of vitality and growth. At Surat, in the early eighteenth century, a further significant schism occurred in the Shvetāmbara sect, under the leadership of a Jain monk named Vīrajī who, basing his views on those of earlier less successful reformers, taught that true Jainism should not admit iconolatry or temple worship. This schism, which undoubtedly owes some of its inspiration to Islam, is comparable on a much smaller scale to the Protestant Reformation in Christianity; it has resulted in the emergence of a new sect of Jainism which has given up the complex ritual dear to the Indian heart, and holds its religious meetings in the austere and unconsecrated *sthānakas* ("buildings") from which the sect has acquired its usual name—*Sthānakavāsī*.

In some respects the debt of Indian culture to Jainism is as great as it is to Buddhism. Of all the religious groups of India, Jainism has always been the most fervent supporter of the doctrine of nonviolence (ahimsā), and undoubtedly the influence of Jainism in the spread of that doctrine throughout India has been considerable. But even if Jainism had never existed, it is probable that the idea of ahimsā would still have been almost as widespread in India as it actually is. It is in other and unexpected ways that Jainism has so greatly affected Indian life. Despite their very stern asceticism Jain monks have always found time for study, and, more than the Buddhists, they have devoted much attention to secular learning. The Jain monk is allowed and, indeed, encouraged to compose and tell stories if these have a moral purpose, and thus much medieval literature in Sanskrit, Prākrit, and the early vernaculars is the work of Jain monks, who also helped to establish and develop the literature of certain vernacular languages, notably Canarese and Gujarātī.

Mallinātha, the author of the standard commentary on the works of India's greatest poet, Kālidāsa, was a Jain. Jain monks also contributed much to the indigenous sciences of mathematics, astronomy, and linguistics, and their libraries preserved from destruction many important ancient texts, often of non-Jain origin. In modern times also Jainism has had some significant influence, for Mahātmā Gāndhi was born in a part of India where Jainism is widespread, and he himself admitted the great impression made on him by saintly Jain ascetics whom he met in his youth. Many factors contributed to mold the mind of the young lawyer who was to become one of the greatest men of the twentieth century, and of these Jainism was not the least important.

## JAIN DOCTRINES AND PRACTICES

The basic teaching of Jainism may be expressed in a single sentence: The phenomenal individual consists of a soul closely enmeshed in matter, and his salvation is to be found by freeing the soul from matter, so that it may regain its pristine purity and enjoy omniscient self-sufficient bliss for all eternity. In essence the Jain teaching closely resembles that of the early Sānkhya school of Hindu philosophy, and it is possible that both Jainism and Sānkhya share a common source in primitive hylozoistic ideas which were widespread in the Ganges valley before the time of Mahāvīra.

The Jain view of life is essentially materialistic, using that word in its strict sense. Jainism, in fact, looks back to a stage in the evolution of Indian thought when it was almost impossible to conceive of any entity except on the analogy of solid matter. For the Jain the soul, called *jīva* ("life") in contrast to the Vedāntic *ātman* ("self"), is finite, and of definite though variable dimensions. The primitive roots of Jainism are also shown in its attribution of souls to objects not generally thought of as living. Buddhism does not allow that plants have life in the sense of gods, human beings, or animals. Jainism, on the other hand, finds souls not only in plants, but in the very elements themselves. Among the many classifications of Jainism is one which divides all living things into five categories, according to the number of senses they possess. The highest group, possessing five senses, includes men, gods, the higher animals, and beings in hell. Of these, men, gods, and infernal beings together with certain animals (notably monkeys, cattle, horses, elephants, parrots, pigeons, and snakes) possess intelligence. The second class contains creatures thought to have four senses only—touch, taste, smell, and sight; this class includes most larger insects such as flies, wasps, and butterflies. The class of three-sensed beings, which are thought to be devoid of sight and hearing, contains small insects such as ants, fleas, and bugs, as well as moths, which are believed to be blind because of their unfortunate habit of flying into lighted lamps. Two-sensed creatures, with only the sense of taste and touch, include worms, leeches, shellfish, and various animaliculae. It is in the final class of one-sensed beings, which have only the sense of touch, that the Jain classification shows its most original feature. This great class is in turn divided into five subclasses: vegetable bodies, which may be simple, as a tree, containing only one soul, or complex, as a turnip, which contains countless souls; earth-bodies, which include earth itself and all things derived from the earth, such as stones, clay, minerals, and jewels; water-bodies, found in all forms of water—in rivers, ponds, seas, and rain; fire-bodies, in all lights and flames, including lightning; and wind-bodies, in all sorts of gases and winds.

Thus the whole world is alive. In every stone on the highway a soul is locked, so tightly enchained by matter that it cannot escape the careless foot that kicks it or cry out in pain, but capable of suffering nevertheless. When a match is struck, a fire-being, with a soul which may one day be reborn in a human body, is born, only to die a few moments afterwards. In every drop of rain, in every breath of wind, in every lump of clay, is a living soul.

Like the monad of Leibniz, the jīva of Jainism in its pure state is omniscient, and mirrors the whole universe; but the soul's natural brightness and wisdom is clouded over by layers of matter, and every thought, word, or action is believed to affect the material integument of the soul. Karma, the cause of the soul's bondage, is thought of in Jainism as a sort of subtle matter, flowing in chiefly through the organs of sense. Acts of selfishness and cruelty result in the influx of much very heavy and inauspicious karma, which results in unhappy rebirths; good deeds, on the other hand, have no serious effects; while suffering willingly undertaken dissipates karma already accumulated. The soul can never gain liberation until it has rid itself of its whole accumulation of karma, and therefore Jain ascetics subject themselves to rigorous courses of penance and fasting in order to set their souls free of the karma already acquired, while all their actions are most carefully regulated to prevent the further influx of karma in serious quantities. Actions carried out with full consciousness which do no harm to other living things and are not undertaken for unworthy motives or for physical satisfaction attract only very slight karma, which is dispelled almost immediately; on the other hand the unintentional killing of an ant through carelessness may have very serious consequences for the soul. Though a deliberate act of cruelty is more culpable than an accidental one, even the latter must be paid for dearly. If the soul at last escapes from all the layers of its material envelope, being lighter than ordinary matter, it rises to the top of the universe, where it remains forever in omniscient inactive bliss.

Injury to one of the higher forms in the scale of being involves more serious consequences to the soul than injury to a lower form; but even the maltreatment of earth and water may be dangerous for the soul's welfare. For the layman it is impossible not to harm or destroy lives of the one-sensed type, but even wanton and unnecessary injury to these is reprehensible. The Jain monk vows that as far as possible he will not destroy even the bodies of earth, water, fire, or wind. In order to remain alive he must of course eat and drink, but he will not damage living plants in order to do so, preferring to leave this to the lay supporters who supply him with food. The monk will not eat potatoes or other root vegetables, since these contain large colonies of plant-lives; he strains his drinking water, in order to do as little harm as possible to the souls within it; he wears a face-cloth, rather like a surgeon's mask, to ensure that he does no serious injury to the wind-lives in the air he breathes; he will not run or stamp his feet, lest he harm the souls in earth and stones, or destroy small insects; he refrains from all quick and jerky movements for fear of injuring souls in the air. His whole life must be circumspect and thoroughly regulated. Buddhism demands similar circumspection on the part of its monks, though not taken to such extreme lengths; but with the Buddhist, the purpose of this is to develop the monk's spiritual powers. With the Jain its purpose is simply to avoid injury to the lower forms of life and thereby to prevent the influx of karma in dangerous quantities.

The number of lives or souls in the universe is infinite. The consequences of this proposition were worked out by the Jains with ruthless logic. Most souls have no hope of full salvation—they will go on transmigrating indefinitely. This is inevitable, for the number of souls is infinite, and however many pass to the state of ultimate bliss an infinite number will still remain bound in the toils of matter, for infinity remains infinity, however much is subtracted from it.

Thus the process of transmigration continues eternally, and the universe passes through an infinite number of phases of progress and decline. Unlike the similar cyclic doctrines of Hinduism and Buddhism, in the Jain system there is no sharp break at the end of a cycle, but rather an imperceptible process of systole and diastole. Each cosmic cycle is divided into two halves, the ascending (*utsarpiṇī*), and the descending (*avasarpiṇī*). We are now in the phase of descent, which is divided into six periods. In the first, the "very happy" (*suṣama-suṣamā*), men were of enormous stature and longevity, and had no cares; they were spontaneously virtuous, so had no need of morals or religion. In the second period, the "happy" (*suṣamā*), there was some diminution of their stature, longevity, and bliss. The third period, called "happy-wretched" (*suṣama-duḥṣamā*), witnessed the appearance of sorrow and evil in mild forms. At first mankind, conscious of the decline in their fortunes, looked to patriarchs (*kulakara*) for guidance and advice, until the last patriarch, Rishabhadeva, knowing the fate which was in store for the world, established the institutions of government and civilization. He then took to a life of asceticism, making his son Bharata the first Universal Emperor (*Cakravartin*). Rishabhadeva was the first of the twenty-four Tīrthankaras ("Fordmakers" through life) of Jainism, and, according to Jain tradition, was the true founder of Jainism in this age, for religion was now necessary in order to restrain the growing evil propensities of men. Moreover, with the cosmic decline, men's memories had become so bad that they needed to commit their thoughts to writing; so Brahmī, the daughter of Rishabhadeva, invented the numerous alphabets of India. The fourth period, "wretched-happy" (*duḥṣama-suṣamā*), was one of further decline, and saw the birth of the other twenty-three Tīrthankaras, the last of whom was Mahāvīra. The fifth period, the "wretched" (*duḥṣamā*), began some three years after Mahāvīra's death, and is at present current. Its duration is 21,000 years, during which Jainism will gradually disappear, and the stature, virtue, and longevity of men will gradually diminish. The sixth and last period, the "very wretched" (*duḥṣama-duḥṣamā*), will also last for 21,000 years, and at its end the nadir of decline will be reached. People will live for only twenty years, and will be only a cubit tall. Civilization will be forgotten, and men will live in caves, ignorant of even the use of fire. Morality will be nonexistent, and theft, incest, adultery, and murder will be looked upon as normal. At the end of this age there will be fierce storms which will destroy many of the remaining pygmy inhabitants of the earth; but some will survive, and from now on the state of the world will imperceptibly grow better, for the age of ascent will have commenced. The six periods will be repeated in reverse order until the peak of human happiness and virtue is reached once more, and the cycle begins again.

In a universe which continually repeats itself in this way there seems little scope for human effort, but though on a large scale the processes of nature are strictly determined by natural law and neither men nor gods can influence them, the individual is free to work out his own salvation. The Jains vigorously rejected the fatalism of the Ājīvikas. It was to a life of earnest striving for perfection that Mahāvīra called his followers, whether laymen or monks.

Jainism differs from Buddhism in that its layfolk are expected to submit themselves to a more rigid discipline and are given more definite and regular pastoral care by the Jain clergy. The layman should in theory spend full- and new-moon days in fasting and penance at a Jain monastery. Few modern Jains keep this sabbath, called *poṣadha,* in so rigorous a form, except at the end of the Jain ecclesiastical year, usually in July, when there takes place a sort of Jain Lent, called *paryuṣaṇā,* which lasts for eight days with the Shvetāmbaras and for fifteen with the Digambaras. The year ends with a general penance in which all good Jains, monk and layman alike, are expected to confess their sins, pay their debts, and ask forgiveness of their neighbors for any offenses, whether intentional or unintentional. This ceremony of general confession and pardon, extending beyond the Jain church to embrace members of other religions and even animals, is perhaps the finest ethical feature of Jainism.

Despite their insistence on kindliness and nonviolence, Jain ethical writings often have a rather chilly character, their altruism motivated by a higher selfishness. The Jain scriptures contain nothing comparable, for instance, to the *Mettā Sutta* of the Buddhists, and the intense sympathy and compassion of the Bodhisattva of Mahāyāna Buddhism is quite foreign to the ideals of Jainism; for an advanced ascetic such sentiments are further bonds to be broken, mere evidence of human weakness, destroying the impassivity acquired after many years of hardship and penance. The chief reason for doing good is the furtherance of one's own spiritual ends. Violence is chiefly to be avoided not so much because it harms other beings as because it harms the individual who commits it. Charity is good because it helps the soul to break free from the bonds of matter. To implicate one's own feelings with those of others is dangerous to the welfare of the soul. The virtuous layman is encouraged to do good works and to help his fellows not for love of others but for love of his own soul; the monk turns the other cheek when attacked for the same reason.

We must not overemphasize this feature of Jainism. Moralists of all religions and none have often appealed to enlightened self-interest as the chief spur to virtuous conduct; moreover, many passages in the Jain scriptures do encourage a more positive and truly altruistic morality. But their attitude is often one of cold detachment which, to the unbeliever, is rather unattractive.

In everyday life the Jains have been much influenced by the Hindus. They often perform all the domestic rites of Hinduism, employing brāhmans for the purpose. They worship many of the Hindu gods, who are believed to bestow temporal blessings, and they have their own versions of the most famous Hindu legends. Nevertheless, Hinduism has made little impression on the heart of Jainism, which remains much as it was over two thousand years ago—primitive science, purporting to give an explanation of the whole universe and to show man his way through it to its topmost point, where the conquerors and completed souls dwell forever in omniscient bliss. There have been no great changes in Jainism over the centuries, and it remains what it always has been—an atheistic ascetic system of moral and spiritual discipline encouraging honesty and kindliness in personal relations, and a rigid and perhaps sometimes exaggerated nonviolence.

## JAIN LITERATURE

The Jain canon, as preserved by the Shvetāmbara sect, consists of forty-five texts of moderate size, chiefly composed in the Ardha-Māgadhī dialect of Prākrit, in both prose and verse. These consist of eleven *Limbs* (*Aṅga*), twelve *Secondary Limbs* (*Upāṅga*), ten *Miscellaneous Texts* (*Prakīrṇaka*), six *Separate Texts* (*Chedasūtra*), four *Basic Texts* (*Mūlasūtra*), and two separate texts which do not fall into any of the foregoing categories, the *Blessing* (*Nandīsūtra*), and the *Door of Enquiry* (*Anuyogadvāra*). The Jains themselves, as we have seen, do not claim that these are the authentic productions of the founder of Jainism, but maintain that the eleven *Limbs* were codified some two hundred years after Mahāvīra's death, while the whole canon did not receive its definitive form until the fifth century A.D., when it was finally established at a council held at Valabhī in Saurashtra. In fact the canon contains matter of widely varying date; it has received far less study than the canon of Pāli Buddhism, and much further work must be done on it before it can be arranged in chronological order. It appears, however, that the *Secondary, Miscellaneous,* and *Basic Texts* contain some material which is quite as old as much of the contents of the eleven *Limbs,* while much of the latter is probably no earlier than the beginning of the Christian era. However, the canon also contains matter with a very archaic flavor, which may be more or less correctly transmitted from the days of the founder himself. The language, allusions, and general atmosphere of the Jain canon show, however, that it is, broadly speaking, later than that of Theravāda Buddhism.

The canon contains passages of grace and beauty, especially in its verse portions, but its style is generally dry; lengthy stereotyped passages of description are repeated over and over again throughout the series of texts, and the passion for tabulation and classification, which can be detected in much Indian religious literature, is perhaps given freer rein here than in the scriptures of any other sect. From the literary point of view the Jain canon is inferior to that of the Buddhists.

There is, however, much noncanonical Jain literature in various Prākrits, Apabhramsha, Sanskrit, several vernaculars of India, and in English, and some of the medieval narrative literature is of considerable literary merit. *Legends* (*Purāṇas*) were composed on the Hindu model, together with lengthy tales of the lives of the Tīrthankaras and other worthies of Jainism. Gnomic poetry is very plentiful. Commentarial literature was produced in very large quantities in Sanskrit, as well as manuals of doctrine, and refutations of the views of other systems. Moreover, Jain scholars wrote treatises on politics, mathematics, and even poetics, giving their works a Jain slant. The total medieval Jain literature is enormous, and is often more interesting and attractive than the canonical works.

# 11

# BUDDHISM

## de La Vallée Poussin

**Buddhism is, of course, well known in the West; though how well understood is a moot question. This selection on Buddhism can stand on its own without the need of comment from me.**

An amazing number of popular or semipopular books on Buddhism have been published during recent years. I am myself responsible for some of them. As a rule these books are built on the same pattern. They begin with an account of the religious and social life of eastern India before Śākyamuni, and then give a sketch of his life and work. Unfortunately the ideas, events, and men of this time can only be known by conjecture, and the reader is confronted, either by doubtful facts and questionable theories, or by a sceptical discussion about them. I shall dispense with some of those historical speculations and biographical accounts, which can be found in so many works, believing that it will be more useful to explain what we know about the internal constitution of Indian Buddhism, and about its changes during the eight or ten centuries of its early history.

The present work deals with the world's debt to India. In writing of Buddhism my first task will be to consider what that religion owes to the land in which Śākyamuni lived and taught.

Buddhism is not wholly original; it appears, during centuries, as a "buddhification" of institutions, ideas, or feelings, which were simply Indian: the asceticism and the clerical institutions took a special character in Buddhism; the Buddha doctrine of transmigraon, of the action and the reward of actions, was a recast of the arallel Hindu doctrines; the cult or worship of Buddhism evolved cording to the general transformation of cult and worship; the elief in a God Saviour, prominent in later Buddhism and less deeloped in early times, reflects also the gradual growth of devotion *hakti*). In short, Buddhism is only the "buddhized" aspect of conmporaneous Hinduism.

It cannot be said that the most notable features of the Buddhist peculation—its "rationalism" (I mean its antipathy to every kind ritualism and superstition), its atheism (that is, its negation of a od creator and providence), its high morality, its pessimism, its nticaste tendency, its mildness and humanity, and so on—are specifically Buddhist.

But, on the other hand, I believe that Buddhism, owing to the olidity" of the Brotherhood, owing to the dialectical strength of s schools, gave to the ideas and feelings it adopted or patronized great strength and *rayonnement*. The common Indian belief in he reward of good and bad actions was enforced by the Buddhist ropaganda. The common Indian feeling of the misery of life, and he general Indian compassion and benevolence, had in the noble gures of the Buddhist saints very suggestive and attractive reprentations. The early brahmanic literature shows that many sages isapproved or clearly condemned social distinctions; but the Budhist order was a living example of equality and mutual esteem. nd so on.

Owing to Buddhism (as also owing to Brahmanism) many old hings have conserved life and even vigour. The Buddhist monastic nstitution of Ceylon today is probably very like the Buddhist monastic institution of pristine days; and this last was probably very ke the institutions of the sects of Buddha's epoch.

## PREFATORY

(*a*) In early India, before the rise of the Brāhman speculation hich is embodied in the treatises called *Upanishads,* Hindus knew nly of gods to be worshipped, of paradises to be obtained through orship, rites, and good works. But there was later a great change. Iany men admitted that paradises are perishable; that the gods hemselves die; that beings transmigrate from the beginning: At ne time they may be men, at another animals; they may suffer in ell, or rise to be gods. There is something better than paradise;

there is a *summum bonum,* a highest good, a supreme happines known later as Nirvāna or Brahma-nirvāna, an abode beyond tran migration, change, consciousness, or personality; technically a abode "supramundane" (*lokottara*) in contrast with the "worl (*loka*), which includes paradises and hells.

This abode is not to be reached through the worship of any go the doing of any good work, the acquisition of any merit, but b austerity or meditation or wisdom—in short, by the discipline lat known as *yoga.*

Henceforth, from the times of the *Upanishads* (sixth century B.C down to our days, every branch of the Indian faith, be it Brahma ism, Buddhism, Jainism, Vishnuism, or Śivaism, has presented twofold aspect. One is "religious," or "mundane" (*laukika*), an deals with paradises, happy rebirths, gods or God, worship, me torious actions. The other is "transcendent" (supramundane, *loko tara*), or "mystic," and makes man's chief object the attainmen through gnosis and ecstasy, of an abode of everlasting, inconceivab happiness.[1]

The difference of the goal involves the differences amongst th devotees. The men of mean aspirations, attached to sensual plea ures, wish for paradises. The "few ones," the "happy ones," wis for a "better part" than paradises: They leave home and practi continence and religious life in order to achieve Nirvāna.

(*b*) The contrast between "religion" and "supramundane disc pline" is a permanent feature of Buddhism. But both the "religior and the "discipline" take a twofold aspect, owing to the develo ment of Buddhology; that is, owing to the fundamental change th the doctrines concerning Buddha and Buddhahood underwe about the beginning of the Christian era.

Our knowledge of the feelings of the early Buddhist folk towar Śākyamuni, living or dead, is scanty.[2] But we feel sure that th general conviction of the monks was that Śākyamuni, no long visible to gods or men, was lost in eternal quietude. A process

[1] The first aspect corresponds to what is called "Lower Hinduism"; the second, to what is called "Higher Hinduism."

[2] I am inclined to believe that laymen and ordinary devotees never thought that the death of the Holy Man had deprived the world of a superhuman protector. But, to tell the truth, we have no information. It is difficult to understand the ideas which found their expression in the worship of relics and *stūpas*—we know that Aśoka never speaks of a "paradise of Śākyamuni" but only of *svargas,* paradises according to the ideas of Hindu mythology.

apotheosis began soon, both amongst the good folk and amongst some sections of the clergy. It resulted in a theory which constitutes the essential tenet of the later Buddhist faith (Mahāyāna): Buddhas, who are many in number, have been men, but their "buddhification" is an event of a primitive age; they are now, as they have been for centuries and will be for ever, divine beings enthroned in the highest heavens. The real Śākyamuni has been reigning for many cosmical periods on the celestial "Peak of the Vultures." The historical Śākyamuni, who was born at Lumbinī, left his home, obtained Buddhahood, preached and reached Nirvāna, is only an image, a fiction, a "created body" of the real Śākyamuni.

It will be easy to understand the profound modification which Buddhist religion and Buddhist mysticism must undergo when such Buddhology is admitted.

## I. EARLY BUDDHIST RELIGION

A number of good *recoupments*—Aśoka's edicts, a few books of popular inspiration, monastic texts relative to laymen, archeology—give an approximate idea of the true nature of early extramonastic Buddhism.

1. *Upāsakas or Laymen.* Śākyamuni came rather late into a world where ascetic institutions had long been flourishing. This explains why the rules of the monastic Buddhist discipline were rapidly fixed (not without variants and recasts), and why the congregation of the laymen—the Upāsakas or "devotees"—rapidly took the form of a *tiers ordre*.

The reader of Kipling is well aware that a holy man (*sādhū*) easily finds food and a roof. But the religious orders, with their little village-convents, could not live without regular and organized assistance: They had official friends, "bourgeois" and villagers, who gave them alms, clothing, houses, and fields.

The "official" position of the laymen is more important than is often admitted. First, they are really "Buddhists," not only generous alms-givers, but members of the Church: A man becomes a Upāsaka by taking liturgically the "triple refuge" (I take refuge in the Buddha, in his Doctrine, in his Brotherhood); by binding himself to the observation of the fivefold morality (I shall not kill, steal, and so on). Secondly, while laymen are under the guidance of the clergy, they exercise on the clergy a right of control (legend or history of the Council of Vaiśālī), and the clergy have to submit to "public opinion." Buddha often says to his monks: "Will such behaviour please the people?"

2. One character of the lay-Buddhism is that Nirvāna is of little importance. It opens the way to paradises or to a happy rebirth as a man. It is sometimes styled *devāyana,* the vehicle of the gods.

By a sinless life, by perseverance in the practice of family and social duties, by benevolence and kindness, by alms to the monks, by the worship of the Buddha and his relics, by the fortnightly fast, a man earns merit (*punya*) and enjoys the reward of this merit in a future life, either as a god or as a happy man.

It must be remembered that paradises (*svarga*) are only places of pleasure and sensual enjoyment. They present no Buddhist features, and are simply the Hindu paradises adopted by Buddhism, but not adapted. The idea that a man might be reborn in the palace of a Buddha, and enjoy his presence, is absolutely foreign to Aśoka (third century B.C.).

3. *Buddhist elements in this early religion.* There is much in this religion which is properly Buddhist; its very pure morality, free from ritualism or superstition; the "buddhification" of the path of paradise, which consists in the strict observance of morality, not in sacrifices; the gods have been ethically improved—they have been "converted" by the Buddha, and learnt to favour the good and hate sinners; the cult of the dead has been metamorphized by Buddhism—they are helped by good deeds accomplished for their welfare by their relatives; there is created a new and very white "white magic": The best defence against evil spirits and serpents is to "direct towards them the strength of benevolence"—"I am your friend, oh serpents" (as in Kipling's *Kim*).

The dogmatic basis of the system is the belief that man transmigrates, that good and evil deeds are rewarded and punished in a future life. We do not know exactly what stage of development the notions of reincarnation, transmigration, act, retribution, had reached in the Kośala-Magadha of the sixth century B.C. But we know that the Buddhist doctrines of transmigration and good works differ from the Brahmanic. Brāhmans have never conceived transmigration as the universal rule: They have always thought that the great gods at least are gods by nature. Buddhists say that the person who is actually Brahmā has obtained this "place" by his good works; that, after centuries, when the merit of his good works will be exhausted by the very enjoyment of the reward, the actual

Brahmā will die and be reborn as a man or a citizen of hell. Brāhmans teach that the good man obtains a happy rebirth, and reversely; but they do not object to the doctrine of "fate" and they attach great importance to sacrificial or ritual "good work." According to Buddhists, "fate" is only the former actions of everyone, and the only good work is the moral act, the act accomplished with the purpose of benefiting oneself in a future life, and one's neighbor in the present one. Brāhmans admit the retribution of works, but they believe that the great god Brahmā is the "retributor" and places beings in a high or a low rebirth according to their merit. Buddhists strongly object to a God, to a Providence: They teach that actions, good or bad, bear their fruit, owing to their own (semimagical) strength. As concerns deities, fairies, and spirits, Buddhism admits not only their existence, but also their power; they are very useful and must be properly worshipped: They care for a number of things too mean to attract the attention of the Buddhist Persons. But they nevertheless hold a very humble position in Buddhism.

It is very probable that these moral and rationalist views have exercised a notable influence on the old India.

Śākyamuni has often been described as a social reformer: "He attacked the system of caste and conquered for the poor and the outcasts a place in his spiritual kingdom." Oldenberg has said in so many words that this description is a misrepresentation. He observed that the man who has abandoned the worldly life in order to be a monk has no longer any interest in worldly or social affairs.

Let us observe that the Buddhist Brotherhood is open to men of low extraction. True, the Buddhists followed the example of other sects. But the fact remains that orthodox Brahmanism scarcely approved this contempt of the caste principle: It condemns the men "who bear by imposture the dress of ascetics and are professional thieves." The liberalism of the Brotherhood was clearly anticaste.

Again, the Buddhist monks became the spiritual advisers of their lay supporters. The moral system they taught contradicts the Brahmanic tradition and the system of caste. Bloody sacrifices are murders; funeral ceremonies are of no use since the defunct is already reborn either in hell or in paradise. Brāhmans are conceived and born like other men; they do not differ from them in colour or physique. The best "fields of merit" (the alms receivers who give efficacy to charities) are the Buddhist monks, not the Brāhmans.

4. *Buddhism owes much to its nonclerical elements.* According to tradition the worship of the relics was at first the business of

the laymen. Ascetics or monks who have in Nirvāna their goal and in the preparation for Nirvāna the rule of their religious life, consider Śākyamuni as the sage who has discovered the Way, no more. The worship of the relics and of the stūpas, all-important in historical Buddhism, has in itself no specially Buddhist character.

Scholars believe that the legend of Śākyamuni—his descent from Tushita heaven into the womb of Māyā, his miraculous birth, the poetic and mythological features of his "conquest of Buddhahood" under the Sacred Tree, and so on—is the work of popular speculation. When we are told that Śākyamuni in his former birth has been the good elephant, the patient bear, the generous King Sibi, and so on, we feel sure that the history of the former Śākyamuni has been embellished with Hindu stories wherein the popular faith had embodied its conception of the good man; we are even justified when we admit that the chief characteristic of Śākyamuni, his universal benevolence, his pity for all creatures, has its origins in the kindly and generous feelings of the folk of Magadha, rather than in the speculation of the clerical part of the Church. For monks Śākyamuni is the "great Ascetic" (*mahāśramana*); India has venerated and loved Śākyamuni as the "Great Compassionate One" (*mahākārunika*). Of course the true personality and the psychological figure of Sākyamuni remains a riddle. His "goodness" was probably fascinating; but India was prepared to worship an incarnation of goodness. The monkish ideal was quite different, an ideal of stoic tranquillity, and the clerical tradition is that Śākyamuni first decided to keep to himself the truths which he had discovered, in order to avoid the trouble of preaching.

5. *Buddhist lay-religion and brahmano-hinduism.* Buddhism was a *pūjā,* worship, also a *dharma,* code of ethics. But it had no rites for marriage, birth, death, or ceremonies for the welfare of the dead. Not that it did not enforce precepts for conjugal morality, for the preparation for death, for benefiting the dead by gifts to the monks and by pious works; but the Brāhmans continued to officiate at marriage, birth, and death; they continued to be the guests at the funeral banquets.

As Buddhism did not impose or even propose any *substituta* for the traditional rites of the family life, it did not destroy these rites or jeopardize the position they assured to Brāhmans. To destroy them, it was not enough to preach that, "although they might be useful for the present life, they are without utility for the next one" (Aśoka).

Brahmanism catered for happiness here below and hereafter. Buddhism professed to be and indeed was much more concerned with the future life; but as an established religion it was deficient in supernatural devices for the welfare of everyday life. Kings, merchants, villagers did not find in Buddhism the manifold contrivances of Brahmanism for victory, profit, or bringing rain. Of course Buddhist women implore Hāritī for children, villagers implore serpents for rain: Hāritī and Serpents have been admitted into the Buddhist pantheon; but they are no more Buddhist for that. The consequence is that a lay Buddhist is not a Buddhist as concerns familiar life; as concerns all the needs of the daily life, he remains a Hindu.

## II. THE RELIGION OF MAHĀYĀNA

1. This Buddhist religion, which until the present time is the religion of the Buddhists of the Far East (Churches of "Pure Land") is generally styled Mahāyāna, "Great Vehicle" (but this term means exactly the form of mysticism described in section IV); it is, in short, a hagiolatry with saints who possess all the power and all the benevolence of really godly persons.

From about the beginning of the Christian era Buddhism had gods of its own (celestial Buddhas, celestial Future Buddhas or Bodhisattvas)[3] and therefore paradises of its own. The devotee hopes and tries to be reborn in one of the paradises, which are no longer places of sensual pleasures, but abodes worthy of their kings; eternal abodes of music, light, worship, and contemplation.

Morality and worship continue to be the chief requirements from the candidate to a rebirth in paradise. But devotion (just as in Vishnuism) becomes more and more important. According to the "low" section of Mahāyāna, a man, even a sinner, is saved and goes to paradise if he only has one unique thought for the Buddha (just as in the Pāncharātra section of the Vishnuist Church).

Chinese translations give dates: Religions of the Mahāyāna cannot be later than the first Christian century, and are probably earlier. The original places cannot be ascertained. But the defini-

[3] The Buddhas are not creators, but they are providences. Mahāyāna is a particular sort of theism. The Bodhisattvas often take the aspects of Saviours. At the beginning of their career they have practised self-sacrifice for the welfare of all beings; later they are occupied in benefiting creatures by every kind of boon. The descent of Avalokita into hell is a well-known topic.

tion of the Buddhas as true living gods is the natural development of the primitive belief in the supernatural characteristics of Śākyamuni: therefore the theist Mahāyāna system probably took growth and importance at the same moment in all the provinces of Buddhist India. The literary testimonies do not indicate the real evolution of the religious ideas, but only the gradual admission by the clergy of ideas probably born outside its pale. It is probable that the Mahāsamghika sect was the first to give an official theology to the adorers of the Buddhas: namely, the distinction between the true heavenly Buddha and his human substitute or avatar. But we remain in the dark concerning the place, the date, the diffusion, and the way by which religious ideas obtained literary and iconographic expression. Art is an important feature.

The problem is the more complex because there are several religions of the Mahāyāna. All have the same doctrine, but the Buddha-God is sometimes Maitreya, sometimes Śākyamuni, sometimes Amitābha, sometimes Avalokiteśvara. Our knowledge of the origin of these Persons (Śākyamuni excepted) is less than scanty. There is some probability that many figures of the Buddhist hagiolatry have been adapted from non-Buddhist beliefs: Many scholars observe that Amitābha, the most popular of the Buddhas of the Far East, bears the mark of Iranism and of the Solar religion.

Maitreya, Ajita Maitreya, Invictus Maitreya, is not a Buddha, but the Buddha who is to come. He reigns in the Tushita heaven, in the heaven which according to an early tradition Śākyamuni inhabited before incarnating himself in the womb of Māyā. Devotees either desire to be reborn in Tushita or make the "resolve" to be reborn on earth when Maitreya will "descend" and become a Buddha. Early Buddhism ignores this "Messiah." He only appears in the latest part of the old Canon; but he is certainly an interesting figure.

In early sources there are two disciples of Śākyamuni, of no particular importance, one named Ajita, the second Maitreya. Later Ajita, *invictus,* is the name or "surname" of Maitreya. The idea that many Buddhas came before Śākyamuni is an old one; the idea that a new Buddha is to come is not early, although it is natural. When it developed the beneficiary was a person the name of whom is like the name of the Vedic Mitra ("Sun" and "Friend") and the name of the Iranian Sun God.

## III. BUDDHISM AS A "SUPRAMUNDANE" DISCIPLINE; EARLY FORM: THE VEHICLE TO NIRVĀNA

1. In the early days the disciples of Śākyamuni who were "men of ascetic or spiritual dispositions" aimed at Nirvāna, or "end of misery," "deliverance from rebirth," the state or the abode of eternal peace which after death will be the lot of the saint, the Arhat.

This form of Buddhism ought to be styled *nirvānayāna,* Vehicle leading to Nirvāna. It is generally named *Hīnayāna,* "inferior or low vehicle," from the designation used by the adherents of the form of Buddhism described under section IV; because these new philosophers thought that Nirvāna (an unconscious beatitude) is not worthy to be sought for, or that the Arhat, an egoist saint, is not really a saint.

This form of Buddhism still survives in Ceylon, Burma, and so forth; it has practically disappeared in the Far East.

We believe that it is early: The Buddhist Nirvāna is nothing else than a certain aspect of the "deliverance" or of the "supramundane abode" aimed at by a great number of ascetics or ecstatics; Śākyamuni is one of the doctors or saints who fixed the practical means of reaching Nirvāna.

In short, Nirvāna is to be reached by the suppression of passion, by ecstatic or hypnotic devices. Therefore a candidate for Nirvāna, according to Buddhist principles (which are marked by a high morality), must lead a continent and frugal life; he must be a monk or, more exactly, a "beggar, son of Śākya." The Brotherhood is one, since it has only one master and one goal; but owing to minutiae in monastic discipline (or to unknown circumstances) it was early divided into a number of sects. Their number is said to have been eighteen.

Śākyamuni's path of Nirvāna is known to us by the canonical texts, which are comparatively late. Scholars are confronted with the same difficulty as regards the disciplinary (or monastic) rules. There is little doubt that the early Brotherhood had fixed rules and was distinguished from the contemporaneous sects; but the disciplinary books we possess are the result of long growth and regularization.

We feel sure that the early Buddhist candidate for Nirvāna must be a monk, a good monk, must practice frugality, continence, meditation on the corpse, meditation on the transitoriness of pleasure, must concentrate his thought and wishes on the eternal peace of Nirvāna. But we also feel sure that the clerical (or scholastical) speculations on Nirvāna and the way thereof do not correspond exactly to the early state of Buddhist philosophy and mysticism. To give an example. A few early narrations certainly prove the habit of religious suicide. Many saints of the primitive Brotherhood "took the knife" in order to reach Nirvāna. The orthodox theory and rule is that "a saint does not wish for life or death," and patiently waits for his natural time. This detail shows that scholars who describe early Buddhism as a "rationalismus" misrepresent Buddhism, and have an inexact (or incomplete) idea of the intellectual and moral "climate" of old ascetic India.

2. It is probable that, even at an early date, there was a contrast between the monks who attached great importance to ecstasy (and to mystic experiences) and the monks who relied on "wisdom." There is a Buddhism centred on the "true meditation," the meditation which destroys the opposition of "subject" and "object," knower and known; this meditation is the fruit of a transcendent agnosticism. There is a Buddhism which teaches that liberation from desire and existence is the fruit of the "knowledge of the nature of things." Both have a long history. We owe to the second a number of theories.

A. *Nihilism.* According to the teaching of many canonical texts there is not in man any apparent principle—what we style a soul—capable of going through successive existences and of reaching Nirvāna. Man, like a chariot, has not any real unity; he is made of pieces (*skandha*): material atoms, spiritual or mental atoms (sensations, perceptions, actions, and so on).

Several theories have been concocted in order to explain how such a "complex" can commit acts, eat the fruit of its acts, pass into a new existence where it enjoys the fruit of its acts. These theories cannot be early, nor indeed is the philosophy of the negation of a living and permanent and free soul. In early days the Buddhists probably believed simply in transmigration and release.

Now this philosophy, according to the Canon, is the truth which must be meditated upon in order to eradicate desire. It is the "cornerstone" of wisdom and holiness. By an irresistible progress it turned into a system of universal nihilism: The material or mental atoms have no more reality than the material or mental compounds. This is "acosmism."

It is well known that the great monist philosopher of Brahmanism, Śamkara, who taught the existence of the Brāhman only and the nonexistence of the world, of souls, of God, has been criticized by theist Brāhmans as a "Buddhist in disguise." And Scholars agree that Śamkara's philosophy is the result of the synthesis of the old Brahmanic faith in an Absolute (Brāhman) and the Buddhist nihilism. Thus Śamkara appears as one of the heirs of Buddhism.

We shall see that Buddhist philosophers also adopted the notion of an Absolute.

B. *Nirvāna.* During the nineteenth century and the first decade of the twentieth, European scholars believed that the early Buddhist Nirvāna was annihilation.

They now feel sure that early Nirvāna was not eternal death, but "immortality," an imperishable abode of undefinable peace, above thought and consciousness. The Canon contains testimonies to this early view, for it describes Nirvāna as "the unborn which is the refuge of what is born," also as the "Immortal element" which is "touched" during trances by the living saint.

But owing to the nihilistic theory (above, A), the Buddhist schools went very far in the way of negation, and sometimes proclaimed an annihilation-Nirvāna.

Some schools preserved the doctrine of the "immortal element," the eternal entity, which is "touched" by the living saint. But they believe that a saint is only a compound of transient atoms and therefore completely perishes at death. The Nirvāna of a saint is only the annihilation of this saint.

Some scholars wholly rejected the notion of the "immortal element" and said in so many words that Nirvāna is only "nonexistence following existence."

A third view is that Nirvāna is eternal happiness; the dead saint possesses beatitude (*sukha*), for he no longer suffers; but he has no feeling of beatitude (*sukhasamvedana*). This Nirvāna is, according to a school of Mahāyāna, the Nirvāna of the ordinary saints.

Lastly, according to the Mahāyāna, the Buddhas have a Nirvāna of their own. Perfectly calm and free, they are in Nirvāna; but they are nevertheless compassionate and active. They do not abandon existence, and will continue forever.

3. It has been said above that a monk is "by definition" a candidate for Nirvāna. But, in fact, Nirvāna, when we consider the majority of monks, is only the ideal of a distant future.

All the immediate disciples of the Master reached sainthood and Nirvāna. But already, at the time of the compilation of the Scriptures, the great object was not to reach Nirvāna, but to enter into the path leading to Nirvāna. A man who has entered into this path must be reborn eight times before attaining the goal. In fact, the only candidate for Nirvāna is the ascetic who practices mortification and penances, and the faculty of *dhyāna* or ecstatic trance, more than are enjoined by the rules of his order, thus acquiring supernatural powers. To pretend falsely to have realized such spiritual progress is one of the four sins (together with murder, and so on) which are punished by expulsion from the Brotherhood. This shows that any pretence to holiness was looked upon with suspicion. We are told that in the early days saints were many and disciplinary rules few; later the position was reversed, and it was commonly admitted that sainthood had disappeared.

The conclusion is that we cannot give an absolute value to the opposition of the monk and the layman, in regard to the spiritual dignity or the goal which they try to reach. As a rule, a monk only wishes to "earn merit" by the practice of his professional duties (abstinence, continence, preaching—the most excellent work of charity, receiving alms, or worship), just as a layman earns merit by the practice of his professional duties (abstention from murder, "home-chastity"—that is, conjugal fidelity—giving alms, worship). In both cases the fruit of merit is rebirth as a god, or as a human being who is capable of entering into the Path that leads to Nirvāna.

## IV. BUDDHISM AS A "SUPRAMUNDANE DISCIPLINE;" LATER FORM: THE VEHICLE OF BUDDHAHOOD

1. From the beginning of the Christian era and probably earlier a number of Buddhist monks came to despise Nirvāna, and entered into the path which had been followed by the man who was to become Śākyamuni, the path leading to Buddhahood. The second form of "supramundane Buddhism" is a Bodhisattvayāna or a Buddhayāna, the Vehicle of the future Buddhas, the Vehicle of the Buddhas, the path that leads to the possession of Buddhahood.

This Buddhism differs from the Buddhism of section III. The devotee no longer aims at Nirvāna but at Buddhahood; therefore, his discipline is no longer the egoistical virtue and impassibility of the Arhat,[4] but the charitable practices of a future Buddha. The

[4] Altruistic virtues have a place in the preparation for Nirvāna, for peace of soul presupposes the suppression of anger, the culture (bhāvanā) of feelings of universal benevolence; but this place is a small and a prefatory one, since the candidate for Nirvāna must destroy hate and love.

Arhat reaches Nirvāna by his own unique exertion: Buddhahood is obtained by personal exertion coupled with the help of the Buddhas and heavenly Bodhisattvas who are living gods.

This Buddhism may be considered as the "learned," mystical branch of the Buddhism of section II. It differs: The candidate for Buddhahood loves and worships the Buddhas and does not despise a rebirth in the paradise of a Buddha (as in section II); but such a rebirth is regarded by him as a temporary stage in his progress towards Buddahood. The devotee of section II is only a *bhakta,* a *dévot;* he is not a future Buddha.

The vehicle of the Bodhisattvas is nothing new in Buddhism. Buddhist antiquity was well aware of the fact that Śākyamuni has obtained Buddhahood in his last existence because during many (552) previous existences he had followed the path of the future Buddhas—that is, because he had heaped up heroic deeds of virtue and self-sacrifice (narrated in the *Jātaka*).

But the general opinion was that Śākyamuni is "exceptional," that Buddhas are very rare.

There was (before the compilation of the *Saddharmapundarīka,* Lotus of the true Law, perhaps about the beginning of the Christian era) a new departure: the discovery of a new truth—namely, that all men can or must imitate Śākyamuni, can pronounce (as did Śākyamuni) the vow of becoming Buddha; in other words, can become "future Buddhas."

2. At the time of Asanga (fourth century A.D.), a monk was always a member of one of the eighteen early sects. But a number of monks, not satisfied with the mystical goal (Nirvāna) and the moral ideal (impassibility of the *Arhat*) of these sects, added to the obligations of the traditionary clerical life (old disciplinary rules) the obligation of a future Buddha, heroic charity, and self-sacrifice; they took the vow of Buddhahood. There was a ceremony, a private one, in the presence of a man (monk or layman) already equipped with this vow.

Later on, as the new spirit developed, as the candidates to Buddhahood became more numerous and influential, the adhesion to an early sect was no longer necessary. A special discipline for the Bodhisattva-monks had been delineated, and they had monasteries of their own.

The chief innovation, as concerns discipline, was probably the prohibition of meat. The worship of the Buddhas, which from of old was admitted by some at least of the early sects, became more pompous and general. There was also a new or renewed spirit of charity and propaganda—a spiritual life more noble, intense, and profound. One cannot read without respect and admiration the formulas of the eightfold supreme worship (confession of sins, and so on) and the homilies on patience, love of one's neighbor, considering a neighbor as one's own self and one's own egoist self as an enemy to be humiliated and destroyed.

There is sometimes much wisdom and moderation in Mahāyāna teaching. We are beginners in the path of self-sacrifice. To save others we must not jeopardize our own welfare. Therefore, we must first avoid sin and exert ourselves in the humble virtues of everyday life; such is the right way to prepare oneself for the heroic deeds of future rebirths.

But this wisdom is not general. A future Buddha must imitate the habit of self-sacrifice which characterized the future Śākyamuni when he gave to beggars or to tigresses his eyes or his flesh—hence, an epidemic of religious suicides. As the Church officially deprecates suicide, an orthodox method of self-sacrifice was created. The initiation into the Mahāyānist community (that is, the solemn vow of Buddhahood) was accompanied by the "burning of the skull" (China). A number of incense sticks are fixed on the skull of the candidate and lighted; the candidate is looked upon as a man who has burned his body for the welfare of mankind.

During all his former existence Śākyamuni was not a monk, but a layman. A future Buddha may be a layman. A consequence of this doctrine is that the clerical life lost its prestige and that Buddhism, hitherto essentially a clerical brotherhood, became more and more a popular religion. This religion was more and more open to Hindu (Śivaist) influences. This is one of the causes of the disintegration and disappearance of Indian Buddhism.

3. The popular and sincere belief in the divine power and providence of the Buddhas was not to satisfy the intellectual needs of the learned monks. The Mahāyāna has elaborated systems of metaphysics and Buddhology.

A. *Tathatā*. The first Buddhist speculation resulted in a nihilistic or quasi-nihilistic attitude (section III); but, while admitting the conclusions of the Ancients—namely, absence of a soul, unsubstantiality of all phenomena (or "caused contingent things")—some of the eighteen early sects and the schools of the Mahāyānist Church recognized an "absolute" which is probably derived from the absolute of the Brāhmans (*brāhman*). There is an immutable element (*dhātu*) below the changing flow of phenomena; more precisely, a "nature of things" (*dharmatā*) or "true reality" (*tathatā*), which is a spiritual or meta-mental reality, a transcendent thought free from the opposition of "subject" and "object."

All beings are metaphysically the *tathatā*. But only a few beings (the Buddhas) have attained knowledge of the *tathatā* by personal experience; they have attained the perfect "equation" of their individual thought to the very nature of thought. This sort of identification is the cause of Buddhahood, is Buddhahood itself.

We are the *tathatā;* therefore, we are Buddhas *en puissance;* we shall actually become Buddhas when we attain the consciousness of our identity with the *tathatā*. It is a long business—a long endeavour in self-sacrifice and contemplation, the career of a future Buddha—to conceive the vow of Buddhahood, to progress during many rebirths before entering upon the first of the ten stages of a future Buddha.[5]

B. *The four bodies.* Early Mahāyāna taught that Buddhas have two bodies. There is a quasi-eternal and divine Śākyamuni; there is a human Śākyamuni who is only a "creation body," a magical contrivance managed in order to guide men towards happiness.

Later a Buddha is said to possess four bodies: (1) a transcendent one, the *tathatā,* the same, of course, for all the Buddhas; (2) the "body of personal enjoyment"—that is, the real thought and form which constitutes a certain Buddha, Amitābha, Śākyamuni, and so on; this body, which is the Buddha himself, will last for eternity; (3) the "body of altruistic enjoyment," the form under which a Buddha manifests himself to saints in the heavens; this body, of course, is manifold, since saints differ in holiness and needs; (4) the "creation-body," the form under which a Buddha manifests himself to very imperfect beings, men, devils, and so forth. The best creation-body is the human Buddha.

C. The Buddhology just described is a compromise between two notions: (1) the early dogma that Buddhahood is obtained through long exertion by beings who have been transmigrating "since a time which has not begun"; (2) the metaphysical view of the universal and immutable *tathatā,* which is the transcendent body realized by each Buddha.

[5] Such is the early and orthodox view, but the thesis that all living beings have the nature of a Buddha could not but result in the hope of quickly actualizing this nature; hence, a number of magical or ecstatic devices in order to acquire the body, the voice, and the thought of a Buddha. See de La Vallée Poussin, *Le dogme et la philosophie du Bouddhisme* (Paris, Beauchesne, 1930).

Mahāyāna sometimes abandoned the early dogma. According to many schools, some of which are certainly old (possibly fourth century A.D.), there is a primeval eternal Buddha—Vajrasattva, the "diamond or the thunderbolt," Adibuddha, the "Buddha of the beginning"—from which the Buddhas issue by a process of meditative emanation; the Bodhisattvas are no longer "future Buddhas" but "spiritual sons" of the Buddhas. Tantric and Tibetan Buddhism illustrate this new aspect of the religion of Śākyamuni.

## SOME REMARKS ON THE DISAPPEARANCE OF INDIAN BUDDHISM

Scholars have given many explanations of the gradual decay and final disappearance of Indian Buddhism. Of course, epigraphical and literary sources are not wanting, and it is not impossible to follow, province by province, the process of decay. This preliminary and necessary work has not been carefully done, and the problem remains terribly obscure. Nevertheless, a few general observations may be useful.

(*a*) For centuries and almost everywhere Buddhism had numbered its monks by thousands, enjoyed the most vigorous life in devotional and philosophical directions, obtained the patronage of kings and sometimes the advantages of being the state religion. But, as we have seen, it had never and nowhere taken the place of Brahmanism.

(*b*) The bonds which for a time strongly attached laymen to Buddhism were the worship of the Buddhist saints and the veneration of the monks—who were not "priests" but moral advisers and excellent "fields of merit."

Śākyamuni has been for centuries a most popular figure. The history of his previous births, of his miracles and deeds, enjoyed the favour of the people at large. Later on, Śākyamuni was superseded in learned and lay Buddhist circles by other Buddhas or saints: Maitreya, Amitābha, Mañjuśrī, Avalokita, Tārā or Tārās. These figures lacked the personal character of Śākyamuni, never possessed his prestige, or, again, had features which established between them and Hindu gods an undeniable likeness.

The presence of fairies and minor useful deities in the Buddhist pantheon was not in itself a great danger, but, with centuries, the Hindu infiltration took a new character. We know that the monks of the conservative party accused their brethren of philośivaism (eighth century A.D.); in Bengal, after the Muhammadan destruction of the

Buddhist monasteries, the Buddhists exchanged their worship of Buddhist figures for the worship of Vishnuist ones; the Buddhism of present-day Nepal is a mixture of Buddhism and Brāhmano-śivaism.

Buddhism admitted into its pantheon and worshipped under the title of Buddhas or Bodhisattvas or Vajradevatās figures deeply stamped with the Hindu (Vishnu-śivaite) mark. Its theology too had been penetrated by Hindu conceptions. One of the favourite deities of later Buddhism is Tārā, "the Star" or "the Saviouress," who owes all her "Buddhism" to her kindness, to her title of "future Buddha," or of wife of a Buddha.

(*c*) The strength of Buddhism is in its clergy, in the Brotherhood. For centuries the Brotherhood flourished in the East, in the Deccan; in the West, in the Konkan and the Telugu country. Buddhist pilgrims and archaeology show the gradual decay of the Buddhist communities almost everywhere.

One lesson of the Mahāyāna (see sections II and IV) is that a layman has the same right to holiness and salvation as a monk: the Mahāyāna to some extent deprecates clerical life. Can we say that asceticism—at least in this form of comfortable asceticism which characterized the Buddhist clergy—was losing its prestige and its hold on religious India?

Buddhists casuists have always admitted that a monk commits no sin when he officially declares that he is not capable of keeping his vows; he then becomes a Buddhist layman and can marry. With the Mahāyāna this casuistry turned into a historical feature. We have evidence of the growing habit of young men to take the monastic vows (a meritorious act), only to proclaim immediately after the ceremony that they renounce the vows of a monk in order to take the vows of a lay Bodhisattva. Kashmir and Nepal have had or have a married clergy.

Another cause of weakness in the Brotherhood was the decline of intellectual activity (already visible during the sixth and the seventh centuries), and the development of the Tantric (or magic) form of Buddhism: pure Śivaism in disguise. The master or teacher (*guru*) who gives the initiation and shows the way to a rapid acquisition of Buddhahood or of worldly advantages is no longer a monk but a *siddha,* a magician, a *vajrāchārya* (often of very low moral habits).

(*d*) The fate of Indian Buddhism must be explained by its own internal faults. At least this aspect of the problem deserves attention. But external circumstances also had no little effect.

The advantage of official or kingly patronage is great. Inversely, when kings were strongly "Śivaizing" (like Śaśānka or the Cholas), or "jainizing" (as in Malwa), or "lingaïzing" (as in the Telugu country), or simply "anticlerical" (as the Hun kings, some potentates of Kashmir, the Muhammadans), Buddhism suffered.

Greater importance than that of the occasional bias of the civil power in favour of non-Buddhist creeds and clergy must probably be attached to the change that Brahmanism underwent during the Middle Ages under the guidance of many religious reformers.

Formerly Brāhmans were domestic priests or held liturgical duties in the ceremonies of the temples, but they had no "cure of souls"; they were not preachers or propagandists, as the Buddhists and Jains were of old. But with Śamkara, Rāmānuja, many other saints, and their disciples, Śivaism and Vishnuism acquired an active clergy. While the vital energies of Buddhism were declining, the Brahmano-Hinduist religion enjoyed a sort of revival.

# 12

# GRAMMAR

## Leonard Bloomfield

In contrast to the preceding selections, the final four selections deal with rather secular matters, even some rather prosaic matters. These selections are intended simply to give some balance to the over-all view of traditional India, to bring into relief additional aspects and achievements of the period that are too often neglected. On the selection on music by A. K. Coomaraswamy, I shall make no comment. It is one of the best and most succinct summations of a difficult topic that I know.

Probably in no other single sphere have Western scholars been so indebted to traditional India as in that of grammar. Bloomfield's characterization of Pāṇini's Aṣṭādhyāyī ("The Eight Books") as "one of the greatest monuments of human intelligence" is by no means an exaggeration; no one who has had even a small acquaintance with that most remarkable book could fail to agree. In some four thousand *sūtras* or aphorisms—some of them no more than a single syllable in length—Pāṇini sums up the grammar not only of his own spoken language, but of that of the Vedic period as well. The work is the more remarkable when we consider that the author did not write it down but rather worked it all out in his head, as it were. Pāṇini's disciples committed the work to memory and in turn passed it on in the same manner to their disciples; and though the Aṣṭādhyāyī has long since been committed to writing, rote memorization of the work, with several of the more important commentaries, is still the approved method of studying grammar in India today, as indeed is true of most learning of the traditional culture. The oral tradition which has preserved so much of traditional India for us is still very much a living thing.

But it is not only the Aṣṭādhyāyī itself that is remarkable, but the whole of the grammatical literature. Pāṇini's work cannot be understood by itself, for most of it is couched in a sort of shorthand or code that the author developed in order to obtain economy of statement. Hence, the grammatical literature is, in terms of volume, principally one of commentary, and an occasional restatement of Pāṇini for a specific purpose—teaching, for instance. Practically all of this vast literature, however, stems from one work, the Aṣṭādhyāyī, which we can date at between 500 and 350 B.C.

The first significant commentary preserved to us is the Vārttika of Kātyāyana, perhaps a century after Pāṇini, by which time the Aṣṭādhyāyī seems already to have been written down. After about another century we get perhaps the most important of the commentaries, the magnificent and exhaustive Mahābhāṣya, "The Great Commentary" of Patanjali. These first three in a long and distinguished line of grammarians—Pāṇini, Kātyāyana, and Patanjali—are known as the *munitrayam,* "the triad of *munis,* sages" of Sanskrit grammar; and by Patanjali's time Pāṇini has assumed the status of *ṛṣi,* or seer. The *munitrayam* are followed by literally hundreds of further commentaries, and then commentaries on commentaries, and commentaries on these again—some good, some bad, some indifferent.

There is no doubt that the "discovery" of Sanskrit and the first postulation (by Sir William Jones in the late eighteenth century) of its relation to the classical languages of European tradition (Greek and Latin) served to revolutionize—in fact, to institute on a sound footing—the historical and comparative study of languages in Europe. But Sanskrit grammar still demands the attention of the modern linguist for still a further reason: not for what it tells us about Sanskrit, but rather what it tells us about itself, as an almost perfect system for describing and classifying language structure; it interests us as a beautiful working model for the description of language phenomena.

While in the classical world scholars were dealing with language in a somewhat metaphysical way (telling themselves what language should be like), the Indians were telling us what their language actually was, how it worked, and how it was put together. The methods and techniques for describing the structure of Sanskrit which we find in Pāṇini have not been substantially bettered to this day in modern linguistic theory and practice.

We today employ many devices in describing languages that were already well known to Pāṇini's first two commentators. The concept of "zero," which in mathematics is attributed to India, finds its place also in linguistics. (The form of the plural suffix of the noun in "The *fish* are biting tonight" as against "The *fish* is delicious" is said to be "zero.") Zero in language description is one of the things we owe to Pāṇini, who recognized at least three kinds of zero. Zero, it might be said is not "nothing," but rather the "significant absence of something." But zero is not the only thing we have in common with the ancient Indian grammarians. Leonard Bloomfield—whose *Language,* published in 1933, remains one of the highwater marks of American linguistics—describes compounds and derivatives in English in the same terms that Pāṇini used for Sanskrit; and, in fact, for the compounds, Bloomfield even gives the Sanskrit names for the English compounds that he finds and describes. Today with all the furore over "transform" and "generative" grammar, we do well to look back to Pāṇini, who does not tell us how to take words apart (to analyze), but rather—an important distinction—how the words of Sanskrit are built up (*generated*) from the elements that are less than words: from roots and affixes.

Pāṇini's whole mode of operation—his attitude, in fact—was not unlike that of the modern linguist: Pāṇini sought and largely achieved what every linguist-grammarian has sought since and what every would-be linguist has had dinned into his ears: *economy.* That is, how to say what one has to say as briefly, succinctly, and elegantly as possible. To be sure, Pāṇini's economy is such that one needs volumes of explication to understand him; and in later times economy becomes a fetish that carries grammar to obscurantism. Still, hardly any linguist today would seriously quarrel with the statement in the (rather late) Paribhāṣāpāṭha:

*ardhamātrālāghvena putrotsavaṃ manyante vaiyākaraṇāh.* "Grammarians rejoice in the saving of half a syllable as in the birth of a son."

Outside the tradition of Europe, several nations had developed linguistic doctrines, chiefly on an antiquarian basis. The Arabs had worked out a grammar of the classical form of their language, as it appears in the Koran; on the model of this, the Jews in Mohammedan countries constructed a Hebrew grammar. At the Renaissance, European scholars became acquainted with this tradition; the term *root,* for instance, as a designation for the central part of a word, comes from Hebrew grammar. In the Far East, the Chinese had gained a great deal of antiquarian linguistic knowledge, especially in the way of lexicography. A Japanese grammar seems to have grown up independently.

It was in India, however, that there arose a body of knowledge which was destined to revolutionize European ideas about language. The Brahmin religion guarded, as sacred texts, some very ancient collections of hymns; the oldest of these collections, the Rig Veda, dates in part, at a conservative estimate, from about 1200 B.C. As the language of these texts grew antiquated, the proper way of pronouncing them, and their correct interpretation, became the task of a special class of learned men. The antiquarian interest in language which arose in this way was carried over into a more practical sphere. Among the Hindus, as among us, different classes of society differed in speech. Apparently there were forces at work which led upper-class speakers to adopt lower-class forms of speech. We find the Hindu grammarians extending their interest from the Scriptures to the upper-caste language and making rules and lists of forms descriptive of the correct type of speech, which they called *Sanskrit*. In time they worked out a systematic arrangement of grammar and lexicon. Generations of such labor must have preceded the writing of the oldest treatise that has come down to us, the grammar of Pāṇini. This grammar, which dates from somewhere round 350 to 250 B.C., is one of the greatest monuments of human intelligence. It describes, with the minutest detail, every inflection, derivation, and composition, and every syntactic usage of its author's speech. No other language, to this day, has been so perfectly described. It may have been due, in part, to this excellent codification that Sanskrit became, in time, the official and literary language of all of Brahmin India. Long after it had ceased to be spoken as anyone's native language, it remained (as classical Latin remained in Europe) the artificial medium for all writing on learned or religious topics.

Some knowledge of Sanskrit and of the Hindu grammar had reached Europe, through missionaries, in the sixteenth and seventeenth centuries. In the eighteenth century, Englishmen in India transmitted more exact reports; round the beginning of the nineteenth century, the knowledge of Sanskrit became part of the equipment of European scholars.

The Indian grammar presented to European eyes, for the first time, a complete and accurate description of a language, based not upon theory but upon observation. Moreover, the discovery of Sanskrit disclosed the possibility of a comparative study of languages.

To begin with, the concept of related languages was strikingly confirmed by the existence, in far off India, of a sister of the familiar languages of Europe; witness, for example, the Sanskrit equivalent of the words above cited:[1]

*mātā,* "mother"; accusative case, *mātaram;*
*dvāu,* "two";
*trayaḥ,* "three";

Even more important was the insight into linguistic structure which one got from the accurate and systematic Hindu grammar. Until now, one had been able to see only vague and fluid similarities, for the current grammars, built on the Greek model, did not clearly set off the features of each language. The Hindu grammar taught Europeans to analyze speech forms; when one compared the constituent parts, the resemblances, which hitherto had been vaguely recognized, could be set forth with certainty and precision.

[1] The words referred to are (with the Greek and Russian transliterated):
Greek, *mētēr;* Latin, *matēr;* Russian, *mat'* (genitive, *materi*); English, *mother.*
Greek, *duo;* Latin, *duo;* Russian, *dva;* English, *two.*
Greek, *treis;* Latin, *trēs;* Russian, *tri;* English, *three.*
Greek, *esti;* Latin, *est;* Russian, *jest';* English, *is* (German, *ist*). *asti,* "he is."

# 13

# INDIAN MUSIC

## Ananda K. Coomaraswamy

Music has been a cultivated art in India for at least three thousand years. The chant is an essential element of Vedic ritual; and the references in later Vedic literature, the scriptures of Buddhism, and the Brahmanical epics show that it was already highly developed as a secular art in centuries preceding the beginning of the Christian era. Its zenith may perhaps be assigned to the Imperial age of the Guptas—from the fourth to the sixth century A.D. This was the classic period of Sanskrit literature, culminating in the drama of Kalidasa; and to the same time is assigned the monumental treatise of Bharata on the theory of music and drama.

The art music of the present day is a direct descendant of these ancient schools, whose traditions have been handed down with comment and expansion in the guilds of the hereditary musicians. While the words of a song may have been composed at any date, the musical themes communicated orally from master to disciple are essentially ancient. As in other arts and in life, so here also India presents to us the wonderful spectacle of the still surviving consciousness of the ancient world, with a range of emotional experience rarely accessible to those who are preoccupied with the activities of overproduction, and intimidated by the economic insecurity of a social order based on competition.

The art music of India exists only under cultivated patronage, and in its own intimate environment. It corresponds to all that is most classical in the European tradition. It is the chamber music of an aristocratic society, where the patron retains musicians for his ɔwn entertainment and for the pleasure of the circle of his friends; ɔr it is temple music, where the musician is the servant of God. The ɔublic concert is unknown, and the livelihood of the artist does not lepend upon his ability and will to amuse the crowd. In other words, he musician is protected. Under these circumstances he is under no emptation to be anything but a musician; his education begins in nfancy and his art remains a vocation. The civilizations of Asia do ıot afford to the inefficient amateur those opportunities of self-exɔression which are so highly appreciated in Europe and America. Γhe arts are nowhere taught as a social accomplishment; on the one ıand there is the professional, proficient in a traditional art, and on :he other, the lay public. The musical cultivation of the public does not consist in "everybody doing it," but in appreciation and rev-:rence.

I have indeed heard the strange objection raised that to sing the music of India one must be an artist; and this objection seems to voice a typically democratic disapproval of superiority. But it would be nearly as true to say that the listener must respond with an art of his own, and this would be entirely in accord with Indian theories of aesthetic. The musician in India finds a model audience—technically critical, but somewhat indifferent to voice production. The Indian audience listens rather to the song than to the singing of the song. Those who are musical perfect the rendering of the song by the force of their own imagination and emotion. Under these conditions the actual music is better heard than where the sensuous perfection of the voice is made a *sine qua non*. Precisely as the best sculpture is primitive rather than suave—and we prefer conviction to prettiness —"It is like the outward poverty of God,[1] whereby His glory is nakedly revealed." Nonetheless, the Indian singer's voice is sometimes of great intrinsic beauty, and sometimes used with sensitive intelligence as well as skill. It is not, however, the voice that makes the singer, as so often happens in Europe.

Since Indian music is not written, and cannot be learnt from books, except in theory, it will be understood that the only way for a foreigner to learn it must be to establish between himself and his Indian teachers that special relationship of disciple and master which belongs to Indian education in all its phases. He must enter into the inner spirit and must adopt many of the outer conventions of Indian life, and his study must continue until he can improvise

[1] Maheshvara, who wanders through the world a penniless and naked ascetic.

the songs under Indian conditions and to the satisfaction of Indian professional listeners. He must possess not only the imagination of an artist, but also a vivid memory and an ear sensitive to microtonal inflections.

The theory of scale is everywhere a generalisation from the facts of song. The European art scale has been reduced to twelve fixed notes by merging nearly identical intervals such as *D*-sharp and *E*-flat, and it is also tempered to facilitate modulation and free change of key. In other words, the piano is out of tune by hypothesis. Only this compromise, necessitated in the development of harmony, has made possible the triumphs of modern orchestration. A purely melodic art, however, may be no less intensely cultivated, and retains the advantages of pure intonation and modal coloring.

Apart from the keyed instruments of modern Europe there scarcely exists an absolutely fixed scale. At any rate, in India the thing fixed is a group of intervals, and the precise vibration value of a note depends on its position in a progression, not on its relation to a tonic. The scale of twenty-two notes is simply the sum of all the notes used in all the songs; no musician sings a chromatic scale from *C* to *C* with twenty-two stopping places, for this would be a mere *tour de force*.

The "quarter-tone" or *shruti* is the microtonal interval between two successive scale notes; but as the theme rarely employs two and never three scale notes in succession, the microtonal interval is not generally conspicuous except in ornament.

Every Indian song is said to be in a particular *raga* or *ragini*—ragini being the feminine of raga, and indicating an abridgement or modification of the main theme. The raga, like the old Greek and the ecclesiastical mode, is a selection of five, six, or seven notes, distributed along the scale; but the raga is more particularized than a mode, for it has certain characteristic progressions, and a chief note to which the singer constantly returns. None of the ragas employs more than seven substantive notes, and there is no modulation; the strange tonality of the Indian song is due to the use of unfamiliar intervals, and not to the use of many successive notes with small divisions.

The raga may be best defined as a melody-mould or the ground plan of a song. It is this ground plan which the master first of all communicates to the pupil; and to sing is to improvise upon the theme thus defined. The possible number of ragas is very large, but the majority of systems recognize thirty-six—that is to say, six ragas, each with five raginis. The origin of the ragas is various: Some, like Pahari, are derived from local folk song; others, like Jog, from the songs of wandering ascetics, and still others are the creation of great musicians by whose names they are known. More than sixty are mentioned in a Sanskrit-Tibetan vocabulary of the seventh century, with names such as "With-a-voice-like-a-thunder-cloud," "Like-the-god-Indra," and "Delighting-the-heart." Amongst the raga names in modern use may be cited "Spring," "Evening beauty," "Honey-flower," "The swing," "Intoxication."

Psychologically the word *raga,* meaning coloring or passion, suggests to Indian ears the idea of mood; that is to say, that precisely as in ancient Greece the musical mode has definite *ethos.* It is not the purpose of the song to repeat the confusion of life, but to express and arouse particular passions of body and soul in man and nature. Each raga is associated with an hour of the day or night when it may be appropriately sung, and some are associated with particular seasons or have definite magic effects. Thus there is still believed the well-known story of a musician whose royal patron arbitrarily insisted on hearing a song in the Dipak raga, which creates fire. The musician obeyed under protest, but as the song proceeded, he burst into flames, which could not be extinguished even though he sprang into the waters of the Jamna. It is just because of this element of magic, and the association of the ragas with the rhythmic ritual of daily and seasonal life, that their clear outlines must not be blurred by modulation; and this is expressed, when the ragas are personified as musical genii, by saying that "to sing out of the raga" is to break the limbs of these musical angels. A characteristic story is related of the prophet Narada, when he was still but a learner. He thought that he had mastered the whole art of music; but the all-wise Vishnu, to curb his pride, revealed to him in the world of the gods, a spacious building where there lay men and women weeping over their broken arms and legs. They were the ragas and raginis, and they said that a certain sage of the name of Narada, ignorant of music and unskillful in performance, had sung them amiss, and therefore their features were distorted and their limbs broken, and until they were sung truly there would be no cure for them. Then Narada was humbled, and kneeling before Vishnu prayed to be taught the art of music more perfectly; and in due course he became the great musician priest of the gods.

Indian music is a purely melodic art, devoid of any harmonized accompaniment other than a drone. In modern European art, the meaning of each note of the theme is mainly brought out by the notes of the chord which are heard with it; and even in unaccompanied melody, the musician hears an implied harmony. Unaccompanied folk song does not satisfy the concert-goer's ear; as pure melody it is the province only of the peasant and the specialist. This is partly because the folk air played on the piano or written in staff notation is actually falsified; but much more because under the conditions of European art, melody no longer exists in its own right, and music is a compromise between melodic freedom and harmonic necessity. To hear the music of India as Indians hear it, one must recover the sense of a pure intonation and must forget all implied harmonies. It is just like the effort which we have to make when for the first time, after being accustomed to modern art, we attempt to read the language of early Italian or Chinese painting, where there is expressed with equal economy of means all that intensity of experience which nowadays we are accustomed to understand only through a more involved technique.

Another feature of Indian song—and so also of the instrumental solo—is the elaborate grace. It is natural that in Europe, where many notes are heard simultaneously, grace should appear as an unnecessary elaboration, added to the note, rather than a structural factor. But in India the note and the microtonal grace compose a closer unity, for the grace fulfils just that function of adding light and shade which in harmonized music is attained by the varying degrees of assonance. The Indian song without grace would seem to Indian ears as bald as the European art song without the accompaniment which it presupposes.

Equally distinctive is the constant portamento, or rather, glissando. In India it is far more the interval than the note that is sung or played, and we recognize accordingly a continuity of sound. By contrast with this, the European song, which is vertically divided by the harmonic interest and the nature of the keyed instruments which are heard with the voice, seems to unaccustomed Indian ears to be "full of holes."

All the songs, except the "alaps" are in strict rhythms. These are only difficult to follow at a first hearing because the Indian rhythms are founded, as in prosody, on contrasts of long and short duration, while European rhythms are based on stress, as in dance or marching. The Indian musician does not mark the beginning of the bar by accent. His fixed unit is a section, or group of bars which are not necessarily alike, while the European fixed unit is typically the bar, of which a varying number constitute a section. The European rhythm is counted in multiples of 2 or 3; the Hindu, in sums of 2 or 3. Some of the countings are very elaborate: Ata Tala, for example, is counted as 5 plus 5 plus 2 plus 2. The frequent use of cross rhythms also complicates the form. Indian music is modal in times as well as melody. For all these reasons it is difficult to grasp immediately the point at which a rhythm begins and ends, although this is quite easy for the Indian audience accustomed to quantitative poetic recitation. The best way to approach the Indian rhythm is to pay attention to the phrasing, and ignore pulsation.

The Indian art song is accompanied by drums, or by the instrument known as a tambura, or by both. The tambura is of the lute tribe, but without frets; the four very long strings are tuned to sound the dominant, the upper tonic twice, and the octave below, which are common to all ragas; the pitch is adjusted to suit the singer's voice. The four strings are fitted with simple resonators—shreds of wool between the string and the bridge—which are the source of their "life"; and the strings are continuously sounded, making a pedal point background very rich in overtones, and against this dark ground of infinite potentiality the song stands out like an elaborate embroidery. The tambura must not be regarded as a solo instrument, nor as an object of separate interest like the piano accompaniment of a modern song; its sound is rather the ambient in which the song lives and moves and has its being.

India has, besides the tambura, many solo instruments. By far the most important of these is the *vina*. This classic instrument, which ranks with the violin of Europe and the koto of Japan, and second only to the voice in sensitive response, differs chiefly from the tambura in having frets, the notes being made with the left hand and the strings plucked with the right. The delicate nuances of microtonal grace are obtained by deflection of the strings, whole passages being played in this manner solely by a lateral movement of the left hand, without a fresh plucking. While the only difficulty in playing the tambura is to maintain an even rhythm independently of the song, the *vina* presents all the difficulties of technique that can be imagined, and it is said that at least twelve years are required to attain proficiency.

The Indian singer is a poet, and the poet a singer. The dominant subject matter of the songs is human or divine love in all its aspects, or the direct praise of God, and the words are always sincere and passionate. The more essentially the singer is a musician, however, the more the words are regarded merely as the vehicle of the music. In art song the words are always brief, voicing a mood rather than telling any story, and they are used to support the music with little regard to their own logic—precisely as the representative element in a modern painting merely serves as the basis for an organization of pure form or color. In the musical form called *alap*—an improvisation on the raga theme—this preponderance of the music is carried so far that only meaningless syllables are used. The voice itself is a musical instrument, and the song is more than the words of the song. This form is especially favored by the Indian virtuoso, who naturally feels a certain contempt for those whose first interest in the song is connected with the words. The voice has thus a higher status than in Europe, for the music exists in its own right and not merely to illustrate the words. Rabindranath Tagore has written on this:

> When I was very young I heard the song, "Who dressed you like a foreigner?" and that one line of the song painted such a strange picture in my mind that even now it is sounding in my memory. I once tried to compose a song myself under the spell of that line. As I hummed the tune, I wrote the first line of the song, "I know thee, thou stranger," and if there were no tune to it, I cannot tell what meaning would be left in the song. But by the power of the spell of the tune the mysterious figure of that stranger was evoked in my mind. My heart began to say, "There is a stranger going to and fro in this world of ours—her house is on the further shore of an ocean of mystery—sometimes she is to be seen in the autumn morning, sometimes in the flowery midnight—sometimes we receive an intimation of her in the depths of our heart—sometimes I hear her voice when I turn my ear to the sky." The tune of my song led me to the very door of that stranger who ensnares the universe and appears in it, and I said:
>
> *Wandering over the world*
> *I come to thy land:*
> *I am a guest at thy door, thou stranger.*
>
> One day, many days afterwards, there was someone going along the road singing:
>
> *How does that unknown bird go to and away from the cage?*
> *Could I but catch it, I would set the chain of my mind about its feet!*

I saw that that folk song, too, said the very same thing! Sometimes the unknown bird comes to the closed cage and speaks a word of the limitless unknown—the mind would keep it forever, but cannot. What but the tune of a song could report the coming and going of that unknown bird? Because of this I always feel a hesitation in publishing a book of songs, for in such a book the main thing is left out.

This Indian music is essentially impersonal: It reflects an emotion and an experience which are deeper and wider and older than the wisdom of any single individual. Its sorrow is without tears, its joy without exultation and it is passionate without any loss of serenity. It is in the deepest sense of the words all-human. But when the Indian prophet speaks of inspiration, it is to say that the Vedas are eternal, and all that the poet achieves by his devotion is to hear or see. It is then Sarasvati, the goddess of speech and learning, or Narada, whose mission it is to disseminate occult knowledge in the sound of the strings of his vina, or Krishna, whose flute is forever calling us to leave the duties of the world and follow Him—it is these, rather than any human individual, who speak through the singer's voice, and are seen in the movements of the dancer.

Or we may say that this is an imitation of the music in heaven. The master musicians of India are always represented as the pupils of a god, or as visiting the heaven-world to learn there the music of the spheres—that is to say, their knowledge springs from a source far within the surface of the empirical activity of the waking consciousness. In this connection it is explained why it is that human art must be studied, and may not be identified with the imitation of our everyday behavior.[2] When Shiva expounds the technique of the drama to Bharata—the famous author of the *Natya Shastra*—he declares that human art must be subject to law, because in man the inner and outer life are still in conflict. Man has not yet found Himself, but all his activity proceeds from a laborious working of the mind, and all his virtue is self-conscious. What we call our life is uncoordinated, and far from the harmony of art, which rises above good and evil. It is otherwise with the gods, whose every gesture immediately reflects the affections of the inner life. Art is an imitation of that perfect spontaneity—the identity of intuition and expression in those who are of the kingdom of heaven, which is within us. Thus

[2] This is like the principle of "conscious control" advanced by F. M. Alexander in *Man's Supreme Inheritance*.

it is that art is nearer to life than any fact can be; and Mr. Yeats has reason when he says that Indian music, though its theory is elaborate and its technique so difficult, is not an art, but life itself.

For it is the inner reality of things, rather than any transient or partial experience that the singer voices. "Those who sing here," says Shankaracharya, "sing God"; and the *Vishnu Purana* adds, "All songs are a part of Him, who wears a form of sound." [3] We could deduce from this a metaphysical interpretation of technique. In all art there are monumental and articulate elements, masculine and feminine factors which are unified in perfect form. We have here the sound of the tambura which is heard before the song, during the song, and continues after it: That is the timeless Absolute, which as it was in the beginning, is now and ever shall be. On the other hand, there is the song itself which is the variety of Nature, emerging from its source and returning at the close of its cycle. The harmony of that undivided Ground with this intricate Pattern is the unity of Spirit and Matter. We see from this why this music could not be improved by harmonization, even if harmonization were possible without destroying the modal bases; for in breaking up the ground into an articulate accompaniment, we should merely create a second melody, another universe, competing with the freedom of the song itself, and we should destroy the peace on which it rests.

This would defeat the purpose of the singer. Here in this ego-conscious world we are subject to mortality. But this mortality is an illusion, and all its truths are relative. Over against this world of change and separation there is a timeless and spaceless Peace which is the source and goal of all our being—"that noble Pearl," in the words of Behmen, "which to the World appears Nothing, but to the Children of Wisdom is All Things." Every religious teacher offers us those living waters. But the way is hard and long: We are called upon to leave houses and lands, fathers and mothers and wives to achieve an end which in our imperfect language we can only speak of as Nonexistence. Many of us have great possessions, and the hardest of these to surrender are our own will and identity. What guarantee have we that the reward will be commensurate with the sacrifice?

Indian theory declares that in the ecstasies of love and art we already receive an intimation of that redemption. This is also the

[3] Cf. the *Granth Sahib* (Japji xxvii): "How many musicians, how many ragas and raginis and how many singers sing Thee?"

*katharsis* of the Greeks, and it is found in the aesthetic of modern Europe when Goethe says:

> *For beauty they have sought in every age*
> *He who perceives it is from himself set free—*

*aus sich entrückt.* We are assured by the experience of aesthetic contemplation that Paradise is a reality.

In other words, the magical effects of a song in working mere miracles are far surpassed by its effects upon our inner being. The singer is still a magician, and the song is a ritual, a sacred ceremony, an ordeal which is designed to set at rest that wheel of the imagination and the senses which alone hinder us from contact with reality. But to achieve this ordeal the hearer must cooperate with the musician by the surrender of the will, and by drawing in his restless thought to a single point of concentration: This is not the time or place for curiosity or admiration. Our attitude towards an unknown art should be far from the sentimental or romantic, for it can bring us nothing that we have not already with us in our own hearts. The peace of the Abyss which underlies all art is one and the same, whether we find it in Europe or in Asia.

# 14

# KAUṬILYA'S "ARTHA-ŚĀSTRA"


## Sarvepalli Radhakrishnan and Charles A. Moore


The following is but a small sample of the best-known Indian work on political theory—though the Artha-Śāstra as a whole is much more than that. Still, Kauṭilya is to India what Machiavelli is to European culture.

One of the four aims of human effort is *artha* or material advantage, which includes political and economic power. The *Artha-Śastra* is a treatise on politics and diplomacy. Its author, Kauṭilya, the minister of the first Mauryan emperor, gives us an account of the law and administration of the Magadha empire. The work is dated 321-296 B.C.

Kauṭilya refers to the views of five different schools on subjects of polity. While both Dharma- and Artha-Śāstras deal with man in society, the former deals with social life from the standpoint of religion and moral order, and the latter from that of policy and utility.

For Kauṭilya, *artha* or wealth is the chief end of life, and the other aims of life, spiritual and artistic, depend upon an economic foundation.

Kauṭilya's *Artha-Śāstra* deals, among others, with such subjects as accounts, coinage, commerce, forests, army and navy, weights and measures, agriculture and law. It also discusses the rules of administration, selection of ministers, principles of taxation, economic development of the country, and the maintenance of discipline in the army.

From Sarvepalli Radhakrishnan and Charles A. Moore, eds., *A Source Book in Indian Philosophy*. Copyright © 1957 by Princeton University Press. Reprinted by permission of Princeton University Press and Oxford University Press.

Though Kauṭilya devotes a section of his work to republican states, he prefers monarchical government. He suggests that the State is established by the weak as a protection against the strong. The king should be vigilant about the well-being of his subjects. "The happiness of the subjects is the happiness of the king; their welfare, his; his own pleasure is not his good, but the pleasure of his subjects is his good." Kauṭilya lays down elaborate rules for the selection of successors to kings and the training to be given them.

## BOOK 7. THE END OF SIXFOLD POLICY

The sixfold policy; determination of deterioration, stagnation, and progress; the nature of alliance; the character of equal, inferior, and superior kings; forms of agreements made by an inferior king; neutrality after proclaiming war or after concluding a treaty of peace; marching after proclaiming war or after making peace; the march of combined powers; considerations about marching against an assailable enemy and a strong enemy; causes leading to the dwindling, greed, and disloyalty of the army; considerations about the combination of powers; the march of combined powers; agreement of peace with or without definite terms; and peace with renegades; peace and war by adopting the double policy; the attitude of an assailable enemy; friends that deserve help; agreement for the acquisition of a friend or gold; agreement of peace for the acquisition of land; agreement for undertaking a work; considerations about an enemy in the rear; recruitment of lost power; measures conducive to peace with a strong enemy; the attitude of a conquered enemy; the attitude of a conquered king; making peace and breaking it; the conduct of a Madhyama king; of a neutral king and of a circle of states.

### *Chapter 1: The Sixfold Policy and Determination of Deterioration, Stagnation, and Progress*

The Circle of States is the source of the sixfold policy.

My teacher says that peace, war, observance of neutrality, marching, alliance, and making peace with one and waging war with another are the six forms of state policy.

But Vātavyādhi holds that there are only two forms of policy, peace and war, inasmuch as the six forms result from these two primary forms of policy.

While Kauṭilya holds that, as their respective conditions differ, the forms of policy are six.

Of these, agreement with pledges is peace; offensive operation is war; indifference is neutrality; making preparations is marching; seeking the protection of another is alliance; and making peace with one and waging war with another is termed a double policy. These are the six forms.

Whoever is inferior to another shall make peace with him; whoever is superior in power shall wage war; whoever thinks, "No enemy can hurt me, nor am I strong enough to destroy my enemy," shall observe neutrality; whoever is possessed of necessary means shall march against his enemy; whoever is devoid of necessary strength to defend himself shall seek the protection of another; whoever thinks that help is necessary to work out an end shall make peace with one and wage war with another. Such is the aspect of the six forms of policy.

Of these, a wise king shall observe that form of policy which, in his opinion, enables him to build forts, to construct buildings and commercial roads, to open new plantations and villages, to exploit mines and timber and elephant forests, and at the same time to harass similar works of his enemy.

Whoever thinks himself to be growing in power more rapidly both in quality and quantity than his enemy, and the reverse of his enemy, may neglect his enemy's progress for the time.

If any two kings, hostile to each other, find the time of achieving the results of their respective works to be equal, they shall make peace with each other.

No king shall keep that form of policy, which causes him the loss of profit from his own works, but which entails no such loss on the enemy; for it is deterioration.

Whoever thinks that in the course of time his loss will be less than his acquisition as contrasted with that of his enemy, may neglect his temporary deterioration.

If any two kings, hostile to each other, and deteriorating, expect to acquire equal amount of wealth in equal time, they shall make peace with each other.

That position in which neither progress nor retrogression is seen is stagnation.

Whoever thinks his stagnancy to be of a shorter duration and his prosperity in the long run to be greater than his enemy's may neglect his temporary stagnation.

My teacher says that if any two kings, who are hostile to each other, and are in a stationary condition, expect to acquire equal amount of wealth and power in equal time, they shall make peace with each other.

"Of course," says Kauṭilya, "there is no other alternative."

Or if a king thinks:

> . . . keeping the agreement of peace, I can undertake productive works of considerable importance and destroy at the same time those of my enemy; or apart from enjoying the results of my own works, I shall also enjoy those of my enemy in virtue of the agreement of peace; or I can destroy the works of my enemy by employing spies and other secret means; or by holding out such inducements as a happy dwelling, rewards, remission of taxes, little work and large profits and wages, I can empty my enemy's country of its population, with which he has been able to carry his own works; or being allied with a king of considerable power, my enemy will have his own works destroyed; or I can prolong my enemy's hostility with another king whose threats have driven my enemy to seek my protection; or being allied with me, my enemy can harass the country of another king who hates me; or oppressed by another king, the subjects of my enemy will immigrate to my country, and I can, therefore, achieve the results of my own work very easily; or being in a precarious condition due to the destruction of his works, my enemy will not be so powerful as to attack me; or by exploiting my own resources in alliance with any two friendly kings, I can augment my resources; or if a Circle of States is formed by my enemy as one of its members, I can divide them and combine with the others; or by threats or favor, I can catch hold of my enemy, and when he desires to be a member of my own Circle of States, I can make him incur the displeasure of the other members and fall a victim to their own fury—

if a king thinks thus, then he may increase his own resources by keeping peace.

Or if a king thinks:

> . . . neither is my enemy strong enough to destroy my works, nor am I his; or if he comes to fight with me like a dog with a boar, I can increase his afflictions without incurring any loss in my own works,

then he may observe neutrality and augment his own resources.

Or if a king thinks:

> . . . by marching my troops it is possible to destroy the works of my enemy; and as for myself, I have made proper arrangements to safeguard my own works,

then he may increase his resources by marching.

Or if a king thinks:

> . . . I am strong enough neither to harass my enemy's works nor to defend my own against my enemy's attack,

then he shall seek protection from a king of superior power, and endeavor to pass from the stage of deterioration to that of stagnancy and from the latter to that of progress.

Or if a king thinks:

> . . . by making peace with me, I can work out my own resources, and by waging war with another, I can destroy the works of my enemy,

then he may adopt that double policy and improve his resources.

Thus, a king in the circle of sovereign states shall, by adopting the sixfold policy, endeavor to pass from the state of deterioration to that of stagnation, and from the latter to that of progress.

### *Chapter 2: The Nature of Alliance*

When the advantages derivable from peace and war are of equal character, one should prefer peace; for disadvantages, such as the loss of power and wealth, sojourning, and sin, are ever attending upon war.

The same holds good in the case of neutrality and war.

Of the two forms of policy, double policy and alliance, double policy—that is, making peace with one and waging war with another—is preferable; for whoever adopts the double policy enriches himself, being ever attentive to his own works, whereas an allied king has to help his ally at his own expense.

One shall make an alliance with a king who is stronger than one's neighboring enemy; in the absence of such a king, one should ingratiate oneself with one's neighboring enemy, either by supplying money or army or by ceding a part of one's territory and by keeping oneself aloof; for there can be no greater evil to kings than alliance with a king of considerable power, unless one is actually attacked by one's enemy.

A powerless king should behave as a conquered king towards his immediate enemy; but when he finds that the time of his own ascendancy is at hand, due to a fatal disease, internal troubles, increase of enemies, or a friend's calamities that are vexing his enemy, then under the pretense of performing some expiatory rites to avert the danger of his enemy, he may get out of the enemy's court; or if he is in his own territory, he should not go to see his suffering enemy; or if he is near to his enemy, he may murder the enemy when opportunity affords itself.

A king who is situated between two powerful kings shall seek protection from the stronger of the two; or from one of them on whom he can rely; or he may make peace with both of them on equal terms. Then he may begin to set one of them against the other by telling each that the other is a tyrant causing utter ruin to himself, and thus cause dissension between them. When they are divided, he may put down each separately by secret or covert means. Or, throwing himself under the protection of any two immediate kings of considerable power, he may defend himself against an immediate enemy. Or, having made an alliance with a chief in a stronghold, he may adopt the double policy—that is, make peace with one of the two kings and wage war with another. Or, he may adapt himself to circumstances, depending upon the causes of peace and war in order. Or, he may make friendship with traitors, enemies, and wild chiefs who are conspiring against both the kings. Or, pretending to be a close friend of one of them, he may strike the other at the latter's weak point by employing enemies and wild tribes. Or, having made friendship with both, he may form a Circle of States. Or, he may make an alliance with the *madhyama* or the neutral king; and with this help he may put down one of them or both. Or when hurt by both, he may seek protection from a king of righteous character among the *madhyama* king, the neutral king, and their friends or equals, or from any other king whose subjects are so disposed as to increase his happiness and peace, with whose help he may be able to recover his lost position, with whom his ancestors were in close intimacy or blood relationship, and in whose kingdom he can find a number of powerful friends.

Of two powerful kings who are on amicable terms with each other, a king shall make alliance with one of them who likes him and whom he likes; this is the best way of making alliance.

### *Chapter 3: The Character of Equal, Inferior, and Superior Kings; and Forms of Agreement Made by an Inferior King*

A king desirous of expanding his own power shall make use of the sixfold policy.

Agreements of peace shall be made with equal and superior kings; and an inferior king shall be attacked.

Whoever goes to wage war with a superior king will be reduced to the same condition as that of a foot-soldier opposing an elephant.

Just as the collision of an unbaked mud-vessel with a similar vessel is destructive to both, so war with an equal king brings ruin to both.

Like a stone striking an earthen pot, a superior king attains decisive victory over an inferior king.

If a superior king discards the proposal of an inferior king for peace, the latter should take the attitude of a conquered king, or play the part of an inferior king towards a superior.

When a king of equal power does not like peace, then the same amount of vexation as his opponent received at his hands should be given to him in return; for it is power that brings about peace between any two kings: No piece of iron that is not made red-hot will combine with another piece of iron.

When an inferior king is all submissive, peace should be made with him; for when provoked by causing him troubles and anger, an inferior king, like a wild fire, will attack his enemy and will also be favored by his Circle of States.

When a king in peace with another finds that greedy, impoverished, and oppressed as are the subjects of his ally, they do not yet immigrate into his own territory lest they might be called back by their master, then he should, though of inferior power, proclaim war against his ally.

When a king at war with another finds that greedy, impoverished, and oppressed as are the subjects of his enemy, still they do not come to his side in consequence of the troubles of war, then he should, though of superior power, make peace with his enemy or remove the troubles of war as far as possible.

When one of the two kings at war with each other and equally involved in trouble finds his own troubles to be greater than his enemy's, and thinks that by getting rid of his enemy's trouble his enemy can successfully wage war with him, then he should, though possessing greater resources, sue for peace.

When, either in peace or war, a king finds neither loss to his enemy nor gain to himself, he should, though superior, observe neutrality.

When a king finds the troubles of his enemy irremediable, he should, though of inferior power, march against the enemy.

When a king finds himself threatened by imminent danger or troubles, he should, though superior, seek the protection of another.

When a king is sure to achieve his desired ends by making peace with one and waging war with another, he should, though superior, adopt the double policy.

Thus it is that the six forms of policy are applied together.

*Chapter 5: Consideration about Marching Against an Assailable Enemy; Cause Leading to the Dwindling, Greed, and Disloyalty of the Army; and Considerations about the Combination of Powers*

. . . By insulting the good and commending the wicked; by causing unnatural and unrighteous slaughter of life; by neglecting the observance of proper and righteous customs; by doing unrighteous acts and neglecting righteous ones; by doing what ought not to be done and not doing what ought to be done; by not paying what ought to be paid and exacting what ought not to be taken; by not punishing the guilty and severely punishing the less guilty; by arresting those who are not to be caught hold of and leaving those who are to be arrested; by undertaking risky works and destroying profitable ones; by not protecting the people against thieves and by robbing them of their wealth; by giving up manly enterprise and condemning good work; by hurting the leaders of the people and despising the worthy; by provoking the aged, by crooked conduct, and by untruthfulness; by not applying remedies against evils and neglecting works in hand; and by carelessness and negligence of himself in maintaining the security of person and property of subjects, the king causes impoverishment, greed, and disaffection to appear among his subjects; when a people are impoverished, they become greedy; when they are greedy, they become disaffected; when disaffected, they voluntarily go to the side of the enemy or destroy their own master.

Hence, no king should give room to such causes as would bring about impoverishment, greed, or disaffection among his people. If, however, they appear, he should at once take all remedial measures against them.

Which of the three is the worst—an impoverished people? greedy people? or disaffected people?

An impoverished people are ever apprehensive of oppression and destruction by overtaxation, and so on, and are therefore desirous of getting rid of their impoverishment, or of waging war or of migrating elsewhere.

A greedy people are ever discontented and they yield themselves to the intrigues of an enemy.

A disaffected people rise against their master along with his enemy.

When the dwindling of the people is due to want of gold and grain, it is a calamity fraught with danger to the whole of the kingdom and can be remedied with difficulty. The dearth of efficient men can be made up by means of gold and grain. Greed is partial and is found among a few chief officers, and it can be got rid of or satisfied by allowing them to plunder an enemy's wealth. Disaffection or disloyalty can be got rid of by putting down the leaders; for in the absence of a leader or leaders, the people are easily governed and they will not take part in the intrigues of enemies. When a people are too nervous to endure the calamities, they first become dispersed, when their leaders are put down; and when they are kept under restraint, they endure calamities.

Having well considered the causes which bring about peace or war, one should combine with kings of considerable power and righteous character and march against one's enemy. . . .

Though actuated with feelings of true friendship, the conqueror has reason to fear his ally, though of equal power, when the latter attains success in his mission; having succeeded in his mission, an ally of equal power is likely to change his attitude even towards the conqueror of superior power.

An ally of superior power should not be relied upon, for prosperity changes the mind. Even with little or no share in the spoils, an ally of superior power may go back, appearing contented; but some time afterwards, he may not fail to sit on the lap of the conqueror and carry off twice the amount of share due to him.

Having been satisfied with mere victory, the leading conqueror should discharge his allies; having satisfied them with their shares, he may allow himself to be conquered by them instead of attempting to conquer them in the matter of spoils; it is thus that a king can win the good graces of his Circle of States.

### *Chapter 17: Making Peace and Breaking It*

The words *sama* (quiet), *sandhi* (agreement of peace), and *samādhi* (reconcilement) are synonymous. . . .

My teacher says that peace, dependent upon honesty or oath, is mutable, while peace with a security or a hostage is immutable.

No, says Kauṭilya, peace, dependent upon honesty or oath, is immutable both in this and the next world. It is for this world only that a security or a hostage is required for strengthening the agreement.

Honest kings of old made their agreement of peace with this declaration: "We have joined in peace." In case of any apprehension of breach of honesty, they made their agreement by swearing by fire, water, plough, the brick of a fort wall, the shoulder of an elephant, the hips of a horse, the front of a chariot, a weapon, seeds, scents, juice, wrought gold, or bullion gold, and by declaring that these things will destroy and desert him who violates the oath.

In order to avoid the contingency of violation of oath, peace made with the security of such persons as ascetics engaged in penance, or nobles, is peace with a security. In such a peace, whoever takes as security a person capable of controlling the enemy gains more advantages, while he who acts to the contrary is deceived.

Whoever is rising in power may break the agreement of peace. . . .

### *Chapter 18: The Conduct of a Madhyama King, a Neutral King, and of a Circle of States*

. . . When, after having put down the enemy, and after having grown in power, a friend becomes unsubmissive, the conqueror should cause the friend to incur the displeasure of a neighbor and of the king who is next to the neighbor.

Or the conqueror may employ a scion of the friend's family or an imprisoned prince to seize his lands; or the conqueror may so act that his friend, desirous of further help, may continue to be obedient.

The conqueror should never help his friend when the latter is more and more deteriorating; a politician should so keep his friend that the latter neither deteriorates nor grows in power.

When, with the desire of getting wealth, a wandering friend—that is, a nomadic king—makes an agreement with the conqueror, the latter should so remove the cause of the friend's flight that he never flies again.

When a friend is as accessible to the conqueror as to the latter's enemy, the conqueror should first separate that obstinate friend from the enemy, and then destroy him, and afterwards the enemy also.

When a friend remains neutral, the conqueror should cause him to incur the displeasure of his immediate enemies; and when he is worried in his wars with them, the conqueror should oblige him with help.

When, owing to his own weakness, a friend seeks protection both from the conqueror and the latter's enemy, the conqueror should help him with the army, so that he never turns his attention elsewhere.

Or having removed him from his own lands, the conqueror may keep him in another tract of land, having made some previous arrangements to punish or favor the friend.

Or the conqueror may harm him when he has grown powerful, or destroy him when he does not help the conqueror in danger and when he lies on the conqueror's lap in good faith.

When an enemy furiously rises against his own enemy—that is, the conqueror's friend under troubles—the former should be put down by the latter himself with troubles concealed.

When a friend keeps quiet after rising against an enemy under troubles, that friend will be subdued by the enemy himself after getting rid of his troubles.

Whoever is acquainted with the science of polity should clearly observe the conditions of progress, deterioration, stagnation, reduction, and destruction, as well as the use of all kinds of strategic means.

Whoever thus knows the interdependence of the six kinds of policy plays at his pleasure with kings, bound round, as it were, in chains skillfully devised by himself.

# 15

# INDUSTRY, TRADE, AND CURRENCY

## U. N. Ghoshal

Because our main interest in India seems to center on her religion and philosophy (and her grammar!), we seldom take the trouble to inform ourselves regarding prosaic matters of the bread-and-butter type. Our picture of India is thus usually a rather distorted one, for one can easily get the impression that India is all spirit and no body. Yet the great empires of all times have had their prosaic business side, without which they never could have achieved greatness, or even survived for very long as mediocrities. Put quite simply (and I don't believe it is an oversimplification), it is economic soundness which, in the last analysis, makes possible the leisure and the security in which philosophical and religious (and grammatical) doctrines can be elaborated. To ignore the everyday, matter-of-fact world of business is to distort the image of a people and a culture. Like any culture, India is as much body as it is spirit; it could not survive otherwise.

The lack of an Indian sense of chronology, of history as such, has already been alluded to above. This selection further emphasizes the point. Note that the native sources most frequently quoted after the Arthaśāstra are the Jātakas. These are part of the Buddhist canon. Essentially folk tales with animal protagonists (the same in many cases that we know from Aesop's version), purporting to recount incidents in previous lives of the Buddha, they are intended for moral instruction. Such is largely the story of Indian history prior to the coming of Islam in the early part of the second millenium A.D.—a reconstruction from religious and other texts.

The Jātakas are written in Pāli, a stage later than Sanskrit in the development of the Indic languages. The Arthaśāstra is written in Sanskrit. Pāli shows, among other features, a simplification of consonant clusters. Note the word *mahāmagga,* "great road," in the discussion of trade routes; this is the Pāli form of Sanskrit *mahāmārga,* with the same meaning (note the *-rg-* cluster simplified to *-gg-*). Note further that the Pāli "guilds" are *seṇis,* while in Kauṭilya—in Sanskrit, that is—they appear as *śreṇis;* the initial cluster of the Sanskrit is simplified in the Pāli.

Kāśi is an older name for Benares (which is now called Vārāṇasī). The *daṇḍa,* by which roads are measured is equivalent to four *hastas* or hands; the *daṇḍa* then is about a yard.

## INTRODUCTORY

The outstanding achievement of Mahāpadma Nanda, the founder of the Nanda dynasty, was the completion of the political unity of Northern India, excluding the Indus basin, but including the Malwa tableland, the Kalinga seaboard, and probably also a good part of the Deccan. Probably because of his low birth, he was led to make a clean sweep of the principal Kshatriya ruling families of his time and make himself, in the expressive language of the Purāṇas, "the sole ruler of the earth." The consequence of this absorption of the petty states of northern India into a large empire could not but have been highly beneficial to the cause of material progress. Northern India, by virtue of its fertile soil and favorable climate, its magnificent waterways, and its extensive coastline must have from the first enjoyed exceptional opportunities provided by nature for economic prosperity. Under the strong and centralized administration of the Nandas, trade and industry could not but advance greatly. In particular, the needs of their exceptionally wealthy court, to which later traditions bear witness, and their organized administration heralding that of the Mauryas must have given a great impetus to industrial and commercial effort. The direct interest of the Nandas in commercial development is perhaps indicated by their invention of a new standard measure referred to in the *Kāśikā* commentary as well as their standardization of the old silver coinage to be described later on.

Beyond the limits of the Nanda dominions lay the Indus, conquered long before by the Achaemenids, but divided at this period into a group of small kingdoms and republics. Politically as disorganized as was Madhyadeśa at the time of the Buddha more than a century earlier, it stood now at a high level of economic prosperity. The accounts of Alexander's officers inform us not only of numbers of rich and populous cities located in the land of the Five Rivers, but also of the wealth of the royal courts and republics. The devastating effect of Alexander's invasion could not but have affected disastrously the economic condition of the territories subdued by his arms, and none of his measures for laying the foundation of an extensive commerce between India and the Hellenistic world took root immediately.

The liberation of Northwestern India by Chandragupta Maurya, preceded or followed in a short time by his deposition of the last king of the Nanda line, and the series of his subsequent victories laid the foundation of an empire extending from the Bay of Bengal to the Afghan highlands and from the Himalayas to the Narmadā and beyond. The military successes of Bindusāra and Aśoka helped not only to complete and consolidate the newly built empire, but extended its limits till it abutted on the Tamil Kingdoms of the far south. For three generations from the time of the founder, the strong arm of the Mauryas ensured internal security and immunity from foreign aggression. Aśoka's vigorous propaganda further paved the way for the spread of Indian culture to distant Ceylon and the Hellenistic states almost to their furthest limits. It is not unreasonable to suppose that these favorable conditions were attended with a phenomenal development of industry as well as inland and foreign trade of the empire under Maurya rule.

## INDUSTRY

The enormous advance of Indian industries which has just been postulated for the Nanda and Maurya times was rendered possible by the abundance of India's agricultural and mineral resources to which the Greek writers allude with evident admiration. "India," says Diodorus (ii.35-37) quoting from Megasthenes, "has many huge mountains which abound in fruit trees of every kind and many vast plains of great fertility—more or less beautiful, but all alike intersected by a multitude of rivers. . . . And while the soil bears on its surface all kinds of fruits, it has also underground numerous veins of all sorts of metals, for it contains much gold and silver and copper and iron in no small quantity and even tin and other metals. . . . India again possesses many rivers both large and navigable." A no less important factor of economic progress noted likewise by the observant Greeks was the extraordinary skill of the Indian craftsman which has been his heritage down to our own times. Thus, to continue with the quotation from Diodorus given above, "The inhabitants are found to be well skilled in the arts." Concrete instances of the skill of the Indian craftsmen are found in the *Geography* of Strabo (xv.1.67) from information supplied by Nearchus.

One of the oldest Indian industries is that of textile manufacture. The technical terms for warp (*tantu*) and woof (*otu*) are found in the *Ṛg Veda* and *Atharva Veda,* while the shuttle (*tasara*) and the loom (*veman*) are mentioned in the *Yajus Saṃhitā* and other texts. Among the textile industries, that of cotton manufacture held the first place. It found an excellent market at home in the habits of the people whose immemorial dress consisting of a pair of cotton garments is referred to alike in the early Buddhist texts and in the writings of the Greek observers. No wonder then that among the presents offered by the Mālavas and their allies to the victorious Alexander was included a large quantity of cotton cloth. While the cotton industry evidently was spread over the whole land, certain centers had early become famous for the excellence of their fabrics. The early Buddhist texts speak with high praise of Benares cloth (*Kāsikuttama* or *Kāsika-vattha*) as well as cloth of the Śivi country (*Siveyyaka* or *Sīveyyaka*). We have a fuller list in Kauṭilya's *Arthaśāstra* (ii.11) where Madhurā (capital of the Pāṇḍya country), Aparānta (Konkan on the western coast), Kāśi, Vanga, Vatsa (Kauśāmbī region), and Mahiṣa are said to produce the best cotton fabrics (*kārpāsika*). In the same context, the *Arthaśāstra* specifically mentions three varieties of *dukūla* (an unidentified species of fibrous fabric) distinguished by their place of origin and their color. These were the products of Vanga (East Bengal), Puṇḍra (North Bengal), and Suvarṇakuḍya (in Kāmarūpa). They were respectively white, dark, and colored like the rising sun. In the same connection, the *Arthaśāstra* mentions linen fabrics (*kṣauma*) of Kāśi as well as Puṇḍra. Kauṭilya also refers to the fabrics produced in Magadha, Puṇḍra, and Suvarṇakuḍya. Linen fabrics (*khoma*) are also referred to in the early Buddhist literature.

It will be noticed from the above that Bengal, Kāmarūpa, and Benares were the regions noted thus early as centers of the textile industry. The technical perfection of the industry is well illustrated by the fact that the *Arthaśāstra* distinguishes varieties of *dukūla* and *kṣauma* according to their color and process of manufacture, while those of *pattrorṇā* are distinguished according to their material and color.

Coming to costlier textiles, we find references to silk cloth (*koseya* and *koseyya-pāvāra*) in the Pāli canonical texts and the *Jātakas.*

Kauṭilya (ii.11) also mentions *kauśeya* along with *cīna-paṭṭa cīna-bhūmija* (Chinese cloth of Chinese manufacture). This last passage points to the fact that silks of Chinese origin competed at this time with the homemade product.

On the other hand, the manufacture of wool was an old and indigenous industry. The fame of the fine wool of Gandhāra goes back to the *Ṛg Veda* which also knows a woolen garment called *śāmulya*. The woollen fabrics of Gandhāra, along with those of Koṭumbara or Koḍumbara—a region connected by Jean Przyluski with the Audumbaras of the Punjab—are mentioned with high praise in the *Jātakas*. Kauṭilya, while silent about Gandhāra, mentions by name (ii. 11) the woollen goods of Nepal called *bhignisi* or *apasāraka*. These are said to be formed of eight pieces, dark in color and rain-proof. What advance the manufacture of this material had attained during the period of the *Arthaśāstra* is proved by the fact that Kauṭilya specifies three varieties of fabrics of sheep's wool distinguished by color, four varieties distinguished by their manufacturing process, and no less than ten varieties distinguished by their use for human beings and for animals. The qualities of the best wool are carefully noted by the author in the same connection. The *Arthaśāstra* also distinguishes in the same contexts six kinds of fabrics manufactured from the hair of wild animals, and differing in their use and qualities.

Before closing the subject of textile manufacture, we may mention a few of its finer forms known at that period. The use of embroidered cloth (*peśas*) is as old as the *Ṛg Veda,* its manufacture according to a *Yajus Saṃhitā* text being normally carried on by women. The *Jātakas* refer to golden turbans used by kings and golden trappings for the use of state elephants. In the times of the Nandas and the Mauryas, gold-embroidered garments were worn by Indians evidently of the richer class. This is borne out by the testimony of Strabo, who says (xv.1.54), "They (the Indians) wear apparel embroidered with gold and use ornaments set with precious stones and gay, colored linen garments." These gorgeous dresses were specially displayed during festive occasions. Describing the festive processions of the Indians, Strabo (xv.1.69) mentions not only the train of elephants adorned with gold and silver, but also the attendants wearing "garments embroidered and interwoven with gold." Curtius, again, in the course of his description of the Indian king's public appearance, says that the king is "robed in fine muslin embroidered with purple and gold."

Wood-work is a very old Indian industry. Reference to the carpenter (*takṣan* or *taṣṭṛ*) and his tools may be traced back to the *Ṛg Veda.* The art of the carpenter had attained a high skill by the time of the Pāli canonical and other texts. There we find the *vaḍḍhaki* engaged in all kinds of wood-work, including ship building, the making of carts and chariots, the manufacture of machines, and house buildings. To the absolute perfection of the craft in Maurya times we have a surviving testimony in the shape of the mysterious wooden platforms that have been recently dug up in the vicinity of Patna. The excellent sculpture of Aśoka's time is admittedly modeled upon the much older art of the indigenous craftsmen in wood and ivory.

Reference has just been made to the Indian ivory worker. The Indians have excelled in ivory work from early times down to the present. Specially, in the *Jātakas* we are introduced to various ornamental and useful articles prepared from this costly material. The use of ivory earrings is noted by Arrian (*Indica* xvi) as a characteristic of very wealthy Indians.

Another industry in which Indians have distinguished themselves in ancient and medieval as in modern times is stonecutting. In the *Jātakas* the stonecutter (*pāsāṇa-koṭṭaka*) is found engaged in building houses with the materials of a ruined village, in hollowing a cavity in a block of the purest crystal, and so forth. The wonderful stone pillars of Aśoka's reign are standing examples of the unsurpassed skill of the stonecutters of the age. "The art of polishing hard stone," as Vincent Smith observes, "was carried to such perfection that it is said to have become a lost art beyond modern powers." The "Mauryan polish" is seen at its best in the walls of the Barabar caves of the hardest gneiss rock, which are burnished like glass mirrors.

The use of deer and goat skins for clothing is as old as the *Ṛg Veda.* The leather worker and his handiwork of various kinds are referred to in the early Buddhist literature. Kauṭilya's Arthaśāstra (ii.11) shows knowledge of a wide variety of skins (*carman*), distinguished by their place of origin as well as color and size. It is interesting to observe that the principal varieties are said to be products of various Himalayan regions. In the description of the Indian dress by Arrian (*Indica* xvi), to which we have referred above, we have an incidental allusion to the skill of the Indian leatherworker. "The Indians," we are told, "wear shoes made of white leather and these are elaborately trimmed, while the soles are variegated."

India has always been famous for its trees producing fragrant wood. Several varieties such as *candana, agalu,* and *ṭagara* are mentioned in the Pāli canonical texts and the *Jātakas*. Kauṭilya (ii.11) mentions five kinds of fragrant wood—namely, *candana, aguru, taila-parṇika, bhadraśrī,* and *kāleyaka*. These are further distinguished according to their place of origin, color, fragrance, and so forth. To judge from the commentator's identification, many of these varieties came from Kāmarūpa, while other kinds came from Ceylon, the Himalayan region, and the like.

The use of metals may be traced back to the Indus people of prehistoric times. The Vedic Indians were acquainted with a large variety of metals—namely, gold (*candra, jātarūpa, hiraṇya, suvarṇa, harita*), silver (*rajata*), iron (*kṛṣṇāyasa, śyāma*), copper (*lohitāyasa, loha*), lead (*sīsa*), and tin (*trapu*). Mention is also made of gold and silver ornaments as well as ordinary metalware. The *Jātakas* refer not only to numerous metals including brass and bronze, but also to the manufacture of ornaments from precious metals and that of domestic and agricultural implements from the baser ones. Kauṭilya (ii.12) specifies the characteristics of various metallic ores, including gold, silver, copper, lead, tin, iron, and *vaikṛntaka* (unidentified). What is more, he refers to technical sciences dealing with veins of ore and metals, to the art of smelting metals, and so forth. In this connection, reference is made to the manufacture of copper, lead, tin, bronze, brass, iron, and other wares. In the following chapters (ii. 13 and 14), Kauṭilya deals with the characteristic qualities of several varieties of gold and silver together with the methods of their testing and purification, as well as the technical processes of their manufacture. These striking references may be taken effectually to dispose of the strange verdict of a Greek writer who, while describing the richness of the country in gold and silver mines, observes: "Nevertheless, the Indians, inexperienced in the art of mining and smelting, do not even know their own resources, but set about their business in too primitive a way."

As regards the period of the Nandas and the Mauryas, we have positive evidence testifying to the skill of the Indian metalworker. From this standpoint the bare observation of Diodorus (ii.36) based no doubt on Megasthenes—namely, that the Indians employed their rich store of metals in manufacturing articles of use and ornaments is not of much moment. More significant is the fact that among the presents offered to Alexander by the Mālavas and their allies were included a hundred talents of "white iron" (*ferrum candidum*). This has been generally taken to mean steel, although Cunningham identified it with nickel. Of the copper work of the Maurya times, an excellent specimen has survived in the shape of a solid copper bolt which was found in the Aśokan pillar at Rampurva and was evidently used for fixing the colossal lion capital to the pillar itself. The Greek contemporary accounts also testify to the precious metal-work used in the royal court. In Strabo's description (xv.1.69) of the Indian festive processions to which we have referred above, we read how the great host of royal attendants carried "vessels of gold, such as large basins and goblets six feet in breadth," as well as "drinking cups and lavers all made of Indian copper and set many of them with precious stones—emeralds, beryls, and Indian garnets." Similarly, Curtius, in describing the king's public appearance, states how the royal attendants "carry in their hands silver censers," while the king himself "lolls in a golden palanquin furnished with pearls which dangle all around it."

The use of jewelry may be traced back to the Indus peoples of prehistoric times. The profession of jeweler (*maṇikara*) is referred to in the *Vājasaneyi Saṃhitā* and the *Taittirīya Brāhmaṇa*. Coming to post-Vedic times, we find the *Jātakas* referring to pearls, crystals, and jewels as well as the art of cutting and polishing gems for ornaments. Kauṭilya (ii.11) shows acquaintance with pearls (*muktika*), jewels (*maṇi*), diamonds (*vajra*), and corals (*pravāla*) of Indian as well as foreign origin. What is more, he carefully notes the characteristics of good and bad pearls as well as the different colors and qualities of rubies, beryls, sapphires, crystals, diamonds, and corals. The skill of the manufacturing jeweler is indicated by the fact that Kauṭilya mentions no less than five varieties of pearl necklaces (*yaṣṭi*) which are subdivided into other classes. In a postscript, he adds that the same varieties apply to ornaments for the head, arms, feet, and waist. Coming definitely to the Nanda-Maurya times, we find that the Indian love of ornaments is pointedly referred to by a Greek writer.

We have not space enough to describe the other industries to which the *Jātakas* and other records of this period bear witness, such as the manufacture of dyes, gums, drugs, and perfumes, as well as that of pottery. But a word may be said about the manufacture of implements and weapons of war. Offensive and defensive weapons like the bow and arrow, the sword and the spear, the helmet and the coat of mail are known from Vedic times. Later in the *Arthaśāstra* (ii.18), we find mention of bows and arrows made of different materials along with different kinds of swords, axes, spears, and the like. The *Arthaśāstra* also refers to two classes of war machines —namely, immovable (*sthitayantrāṇi*) and movable (*calayantrāṇi*), the first consisting of ten and the second of seventeen named varieties. The Greek accounts relating specifically to the Nanda-Maurya times bear out these observations. According to Arrian (*Indica* xvi), the Indian foot soldiers were armed with bows and javelins as well as broad-bladed swords, while the horsemen carried two lances. In the list of presents offered by the Mālavas and their allies to Alexander were included 1050 (or, according to another account, 500) four-horsed chariots and 1000 bucklers.

## TRADE

By the time of the early Buddhist literature, the Indians had developed an extensive system of inland trade which was borne along well-known trade routes. These routes were marked by convenient stages and served to link up the most distant parts of the country with one another. Among them we may mention specifically the following:

1. East to west. This most important route ran principally along the great rivers. From Champā boats plied up to Benares, the great industrial and trading center of those times. From Benares they led up the Ganges as far as Sahajāti and up the Jumna as far as Kauśāmbī. Further west the route led by land tracts to Sindhu, famous for its breed of horses, and Sauvīra ("Sophir" or "Ophir" of the Old Testament?).
2. North to southwest. This route extended from Srāvastī, the famous capital of Kosala, to Pratiṣṭhāna on the Godāvarī and the stations lying on it in the reverse direction included Ujjayinī, Vidiśā, and Kauśāmbī.
3. North to southeast. Along this route which ran from Śrāvastī to Rājagṛha lay a number of stations including Kapilavastu, Vaiśālī, Pāṭaliputra, and Nālandā.
4. Northwest route, also referred to by Pāṇini. It stretched along the land of the Five Rivers to the great highways of Central and Western Asia.

We also hear of merchants traveling from Kashmir and Gandhāra to Videha, from Benares to Ujjayinī, from Magadha to Sauvīra, and so forth. What vast wealth accrued from this system of inland trade is illustrated by references to merchant princes like Anāthapiṇḍika of Śrāvastī, whose trading connections extended to Rājagṛha on the one side and Kāśī on the other. Nevertheless, the path of the trader was anything but easy. Not only were the roads (especially through the forests) infested by robbers against whom the merchants protected themselves by hiring the services of forest-guards, but the deserts had to be crossed at night with the help of land pilots (*thala-niyāmaka*) guiding the caravan by the stars. Associated with the wilderness was a host of real and imaginary dangers—namely, drought, famine, wild beasts, robbers, and demons. Some of the roads were already distinguished as "royal" or "great" roads (*rāja-patha* or *mahāmagga*), unlike the ordinary bypaths (*upapatha*). But the rivers were not bridged and had to be crossed by ferries. The overland as well as oversea trade likewise attracted the attention of Indian merchants. The Pāli canonical texts speak of voyages lasting six months in ships (*nāvā*) which could be drawn up on shore in the winter. The *Jātakas,* above all, have preserved memories of voyages of daring Indian merchants beyond the seas and lands to distant countries of the east and west. References are made in these works to merchants voyaging from Champā or even Benares to the mysterious land of Suvarṇabhūmi, Burma, the Malay Peninsula, and the Malay Archipelago. We hear even of merchants voyaging from the great western seaport of Bharukaccha to the same destination, obviously via a Ceylonese port. Indeed, Ceylon (Tambapaṇṇi) at that time was "another bourne of oversea commerce." We also learn how another body of merchants traveled from Benares to Bāveru (Babylon). An interesting sidelight is thrown upon the methods of Indian navigation by the reference to the direction-giving crows (*disā-kāka*), showing the navigators as they flew towards the land in what direction lay the coast. This practice, as has been remarked, was also known to the seafaring Babylonians and Phoenicians of early times.

The references in Kauṭilya's *Arthaśāstra,* scattered and incidental as they are, register some advance in the conditions of trade above described. Active encouragement of trade on the part of the State is proved by the care with which Kauṭilya provides for the construction and security of trade routes and the foundation of market towns in his scheme of State colonization of the country part. Elsewhere (ii.4), the largest scale of width—eight *daṇḍas* as compared with the usual four *daṇḍas*—is prescribed for roads leading to the market towns (*saṃyānīya patha*). Intelligent appreciation of the importance of trade routes is shown by the discussion in *Arthaśāstra* circles (vii.12) of the relative advantages of different types of trade routes from the standpoint of their conduciveness to commerce. Such are the pairs: land and water routes, water routes along the coast and through mid-water, the Himalayan and the southern land routes. In comparing the last pair, the *Arthaśāstra* authors give us a valuable, though far from exhaustive, list of the imports borne along both routes evidently to the Ganges valley. According to an unnamed teacher quoted by Kauṭilya, the costlier merchandise consisting of elephants, horses, fragrant products, tusks, skins, gold, and silver were more plentiful in the Himalayas. In Kauṭilya's opinion, on the other hand, the merchandise other than blankets, skins, and horses, and consisting of conch shells, diamonds, jewels, pearls, and gold, was more plentiful in the south. For the rest, the remarkable lists of agricultural, manufacturing, and other products of different lands which Kauṭilya mentions (ii.11-12) testify to the extent, as well as the objects, of India's internal and foreign trade. Among these products are found textiles of Bengal, Assam, Benares, the Konkan, and Pāṇḍya; the silks of China; the woollens of Nepal; the skins of the Himalayan regions; the fragrant wood of Assam, Ceylon, and the Himalayas; the gems of Ceylon, Alakanda, and Vivarna (unidentified); and the like.

All the indications point to the fact that the rise of the Nandas and the Mauryas helped greatly to improve India's inland and foreign trade. The liberation of the Indus valley, and still more the repulse of Seleucus, gave Chandragupta Maurya complete control over the coveted northwestern route to which we have referred above. With the conquest of the Deccan by Chandragupta Maurya or Bindusāra, the possession of the equally, or still more, valuable western and southern routes was ensured to the Mauryas. The conquest of Kalinga by Aśoka destroyed the only possible rival for the mastery of the eastern trade. While the Mauryas thus brought all the great inland trade routes under the control of a highly centralized and efficient administration, their rule was helpful for the growth of trade in other ways. That the Mauryas had a special department for the construction of roads is proved by Megasthenes' reference (quoted, Strabo, xv.1.50) to the duties of officers called *Agoranomoi* ("market commissioners"). They had, among other duties, to "construct roads and at every ten *stadia* set up a pillar to show the byroads and distances." The most renowned of the imperial roads of these times was the "Royal Road" connecting the northwest frontier with Pāṭaliputra and leading thence to the mouths of the Ganges. The stages of this first Indian Grand Trunk Road, together with their distances, have been recorded by the Roman writer Pliny in his encyclopaedic work called *Natural History* (vi.21).

We have reasons to believe that the ancient foreign trade of India, like its inland trade, benefited by the strong and efficient administration of the Mauryas. The wise policy of friendship with the Hellenistic powers started by Chandragupta Maurya after the repulse of Seleucus and maintained by his son and grandson, must have favored the expansion of the Indian trade with West Asia and Egypt. It is interesting to learn from Greek classical sources that the main commerce between the early Seleucid Empire and India was borne partly by the land route (the northern one passing through Bactria and the southern through Gedrosia and Carmania, Persis, and Susiana) and partly by the sea route (through Gerrha on the west coast of the Persian Gulf). Like the Indian route to Egypt stretching along the east shore of the Red Sea, the route through the Persian Gulf was controlled by powerful Arab tribes engaged in a highly developed trade. How valuable was this western trade to India will appear from the list of her exports into Egypt, which, according to Greek classical sources, consisted of ivory, tortoise shell, pearls, pigments, and dyes (specially indigo), nard, costum, malabathron, and rare woods. It is probably in the light of this extensive commerce with Western lands that we have to understand Aśoka's ambitious attempt to extend the benefits of his religious and humanitarian propaganda to the Hellenistic kingdoms almost to their furthest limits. To the mutual knowledge and understanding derived from long, continued commercial intercourse, again, we may probably attribute the success which attended Aśoka's mission to Ceylon and, if this can be taken to be authentic, the mission of Soṇa and Uttara to Suvaṇṇabhūmi (Further India).

## THE ORGANIZATION OF INDUSTRY AND TRADE

The organization of crafts and trades in some forms of association was known from early times. Insofar as the crafts are concerned, we find in the *Jātakas* that sons ordinarily, if not invariably, followed the occupations of their fathers, while the industries used to be localized in towns and villages, and the separate crafts had frequently a *pamukha* (president) or *jeṭṭha* (alderman) presiding over them. These three features, as Fick observed long ago, point to an organization similar to that of the craft-guilds in medieval Europe. The *Jātakas* in fact refer to eighteen *seṇis* (guilds), mentioning four by name: those of woodcutters, smiths, leather dressers, and painters. As regards the organization of trade, the *Jātakas* refer to *satthavāhas,* whose directions were obeyed by the caravans along the trade routes, as well as to *pamukhas* and *jeṭṭhas* of the separate trades. We also hear of disputes between guilds being decided by a *mahāseṭṭhi,* who acted practically as "chief alderman over the aldermen of the guilds." The early *Dharmaśāstras* and the *Arthaśāstra* register a somewhat advanced stage of development. From an oft-quoted passage (xi.1) of Gautama's *Dharmasūtra,* supposed to be the oldest of the existing *Dharmasūtras,* we learn that traders and artisans along with others had the authority to lay down rules for their respective classes. Of the *Saṃghas* (corporations) described by Kauṭilya (xi.1), who were ruled by *mukhyas* ("executive officers"), one class consisted of certain specified and unspecified groups living by *vārtā* (agriculture, cattle breeding, and trade) as well as by *śastra* (fighting). Elsewhere (ii.7, iii.1, viii.4, and so on) Kauṭilya refers to *śreṇīs* (guilds) organized under *mukhyas,* which were thought to be sufficiently important for their customs to be recorded in official registers and were otherwise a factor to be reckoned with in the working of the State administration.

The industrial and commercial *śreṇīs* and *saṃghas* we have described above represent the type of guild organization under which there could be little scope of a separate class of wage earners as distinguished from producers. But already in these times we hear of another type of organization involving the employment of hired laborers by the capitalists. The *Jātakas* make frequent references to free laborers working for hire (*kammakara* and *bhatakas*) often along with slaves (*dāsas*) and servants (*pessas*). Kauṭilya (iii.13-14) not only refers to free laborers (*karmakaras* and *bhṛtakas*) along with slaves (*dāsas*), but gives a whole body of laws for regulating their work and wages. That the free laborers along with slaves formed an important element of the population in Maurya times is proved by Aśoka's including the kind treatment of *dāsas* and *bhatakas* among the constituent qualities of his *dhamma* (Rock Edicts ix, xi, and so on).

## STATE INDUSTRIAL AND COMMERCIAL POLICY

No account of the economic conditions of the Nanda-Maurya times will be complete without some reference to the policy pursued by the State in relation to industry and trade. We may begin by noticing some features of the traditional policy in these respects as reflected in the *Arthaśāstra*. That the active encouragement of industry and commerce was contemplated as a duty of the State is illustrated by the measures included in Kauṭilya's scheme of State colonization of rural areas (ii.1): They include the working of mines and forests, the construction and security of trade routes, and the foundation of market towns. In this connection the king is enjoined to secure trade routes from obstruction by his favorites (*vallabhas*), officers (*kārmikas*), and frontier guards (*anta-pālas*) as well as by thieves and animal herds—a list sufficiently instructive as putting the danger from the King's officers on a level with that caused by thieves and animals. How fully the industrial and commercial classes were associated with the royal court and capital is proved by the immediately following rules (ii.4) relating to the planned settlement of the fortified capital (*durga*). According to this description which, by the way, illustrates the relative social status of different groups of artisans and traders in the times concerned. The dealers in scents, garlands, paddy, and so forth, and the chief artisans should live along with the Kshatriyas to the east of the royal palace. The dealers in cooked food, liquors, and flesh should live along with Vaiśyas to the south. The manufacturers of woollen and cotton goods, the armor makers, and so forth, should live along with Śūdras on the west. The manufacturers of base metals and precious stones should live along with the Brāhmins on the north.

Not only did the State associate itself closely with the trading and industrial classes, but it also undertook manufactures and trading on its own account. What is more, the rules of the *Arthaśāstra* repeatedly show how thoroughly the agricultural, mineral, and other resources of the State were understood to be the sources of its strength. Thus among the qualities of a good country are included (vi.1) the possession of agricultural tracts, mines, forests of various kinds, land and waterways, and the like. Very characteristic, again, is the general rule of foreign policy (vii.1) stating that the king should follow that one of the sixfold forms by which he can exploit his own mines and forests and obstruct those of his enemy. No wonder, then, that the nice balancing of the advantages of working tracts rich in mines and in food grains, of working mines yielding a precious but small output and those producing inferior but large output, of working trade routes by land and water, and so forth, formed the subject of keen discussion in *Arthaśāstra* circles dealing with questions of foreign policy (vii.11-12).

Another aspect of State industrial policy in these times is that relating to the strict control of artisans and traders. We have in the *Arthaśāstra* a whole section (Section iv) significantly called *"Removal of Thorns" (kaṇṭaka śodhanam)*, which describes successively the measures to be taken by the king for securing the people against artisans and merchants, against natural calamities, against persons living by clandestine means, and so forth. In thorough accord with this attitude is that fact that elsewhere (iv.1), Kauṭilya characterizes merchants, artisans, and some other specified classes as thieves in fact, though not in name. In the class of artisans just mentioned are included weavers, washermen, goldsmiths, workers in copper and other metals, physicians, actors, minstrels, and beggars. How drastically paternal the State regulations for protection of the public against these classes sometimes might be is proved by a number of examples. Not only is a differential scale of wages fixed for weaving different kinds of cloth, but fines and other penalties are prescribed for reduction in their weight and measures. Fines are also prescribed for washermen washing clothes elsewhere than on wooden planks or on smooth stone, for wearing clothes other than those marked with a cudgel, for selling, mortgaging, or hiring clothes of others, and even for delay in returning the clothes. Wages at varying rates are laid down for dyeing different qualities of cloth. A scale of penalties is laid down for physicians failing in or neglecting the treatment of diseases.

The measures for public security (iv.2) against traders partake of the same character. We read that such old wares as are of proved ownership should be sold or mortgaged at the market place (*paṇya-saṃsthā*) under supervision of the market superintendent (*saṃsthā-dhyakṣa*). A graduated scale of fines is prescribed for deficiency in weight and measures. There is a similar scale of fines for exceeding the profit limit of five per cent permitted on home-grown merchandise and of ten per cent allowed on foreign merchandise. In a later chapter of the same section (iv.4) dealing with lost and stolen property, we are pointedly told that the sale or mortgage of old wares should not be carried out without informing the market superintendent. It is characteristic of Kauṭilya's attitude towards traders (*vaidehaka*) that, unlike an unnamed *Arthaśāstra* authority whom he quotes, he thinks (viii.4) the oppression from traders to be worse even than that caused by the Guardian of the Frontier (*antapāla*).

On the other hand, it is only fair to add that the State in these times also took special steps to protect the artisans and merchants. For theft of small articles belonging to artisans and craftsmen, Kauṭilya prescribes (iv.10) fines as high as 100 *paṇas*. Elsewhere (iv.13) he lays down elaborate rules for compensating merchants (*sārthika*) for theft or robbery of their merchandise during their journeys.

The Mauryas followed the traditional State policy in relation to industry and trade at least in some important respects. We have already seen what care they bestowed upon the construction of roads through a special class of officers called *Agoranomoi* by Megasthenes. That they established State manufactures on their own account is proved by Megasthenes' reference to his fourth Indian caste—namely, that of artisans. Speaking of this class, Diodorus (ii.41) says that they were not only exempted from paying taxes, but even received maintenance from the Royal exchequer. More guardedly, Arrian (*Indica,* xii) states that while handicraftsmen and retail dealers pay tribute, an exception is made in favor of makers of weapons of war, ship builders, and sailors, who even draw pay from the State. Evidently the artisans maintained by the State were employed on government service. What strict control was maintained by the Maurya government over the artisans and merchants alike of the countryside and of the capital is proved by other statements of Megasthenes. We learn that the *Agoranomoi* had, among other duties, to superintend crafts connected with land, such as those of woodcutters, carpenters, blacksmiths, and miners. Again, the officers known as *Astynomoi* ("city commissioners") were divided into six boards. Of these the fourth "is that which has to do with sales and barter, and these look after the measure, and the fruits of the season, that the latter may be sold by stamp"; the fifth "is that of those who have charge of the works made by artisans and sell these by stamps, the new apart from the old." We have elsewhere given reasons for identifying Megasthenes' officers in charge of measures with Kauṭilya's *pautavādhyakṣa* ("superintendent of weights and measures") and *saṃsthādhyakṣa* ("market superintendent"), while connecting "the stamp" mentioned by the Greek writer with the *abhijñāna-mudrā,* which according to *Arthaśāstra* (ii.27) was given by the *antapāla* to incoming traders. We have finally to mention in the present place another reference suggesting that the person of the artisans was protected by a special law unlike the general rule of law known to the *Arthaśāstra.* According to Strabo (xv.1.54), if a person caused the loss of a hand or an eye to a craftsman, he was put to death. This is a severe departure from the milder rule of law in the *Arthaśāstra* (iii.19) imposing fines alone for the same offences.

## CURRENCY

Long before the rise of the Nandas and the Mauryas, India had evolved her own monetary system based on the indigenous standards. The Vedic *niṣka, śatamāna,* and *suvarṇa* may have been ingots of gold of definite weights. But in later works such as the *Jātakas,* the grammar of Pāṇini, and the *Arthaśāstra* of Kauṭilya, we have definite reference to gold coins called *niṣka* and *suvarṇa,* silver coins called *kārṣāpaṇas* or *dharaṇas,* and copper coins also called *kārṣāpaṇas,* along with their multiples and subdivisions. The Vedic *śatamāna,* as its name implies, was based on the *māna* unit, a weight known to the *Ṛg Veda.* In later times the *māna* was changed for the lighter unit called *kṛṣṇala* or *rati,* the seed of the *guñja* berry. The weight of the gold *suvarṇa* in the *Arthaśāstra* as well as in Manu and Yājñavalkya is given as 80 *guñjas* or *ratis,* the copper *kārṣāpaṇa* according to Manu and Yājñavalkya also weighing 80 *ratis.* The weight of the silver *dharaṇas* in the *Arthaśāstra,* however, amounts very nearly to 80 *ratis,* while in Manu and Yājñavalkya it is only 32 *ratis.* As Professor Rapson has well observed, the silver and copper coinages in Ancient India were often independent of each other, with different areas of circulation. In the Arthaśāstra, however, the silver *paṇa* is evidently recognized as the standard coin, while the copper *māṣaka* with its divisions ranks as a token currency. Apparently copper was linked up with silver in such a way that the *māṣaka* was one-sixteenth in value of the silver *paṇa,* its weight varying with the ratio between the two metals.

The punch-marked silver coins that have been found in large numbers all over India have been identified on all hands with the silver *kārṣāpaṇas, dharaṇas,* or *purāṇas* of the Smṛtis and the *Arthaśāstra.* Some classes of these coins have been traced back to pre-Mauryan times. Thus a distinctive class of such coins, which was found some years ago in a deposit at Paila in the Kheri district of the Uttar Pradesh, has been generally identified as the local currency of the independent Kosala kingdom before its absorption by Magadha. These coins bear four obverse marks instead of the usual five, among which is included the four-spoked wheel in place of the usual five-spoked one. They are of the reduced standard of 24 to 30 *ratis* in place of the theoretical 32 *ratis*. Of the punch-marked silver coins bearing the usual number of five obverse marks, two distinct classes assignable to as many distinct periods have been recovered from recent excavations on the site of Taxila. The Older Class is dated circa 317 B.C. by the presence in its midst of gold coins of Alexander and his half-brother Philip Arrhidaeus "in mint condition," while the date of the Later Class is fixed at circa 248 B.C. by the occurrence of a coin of Diodotus in the same deposit. The two classes are distinguished from each other by their fabric as well as symbols, though equally approximating to the standard of 32 *ratis*. The Older (pre-Maurya) Class consists of large thin pieces unlike the small thick coins of the Later (Maurya) Class. The obverse marks of the Older Class are conspicuously lacking in the distinctive Maurya symbols ("hill and crescent" as well as "peacock"). It seems to be generally agreed that some of the coins of the Older Class go back to the fourth or even the fifth century B.C. On the other hand, it must be admitted that the symbolism and metrology of the silver punch-marked coins are still an unsolved problem.

In circulation with the Older Class of silver coins just described, though probably dating from much earlier times, was a class of coins consisting of thick, slightly bent bars of silver with "the six-armed symbol" on the obverse and a blank reverse. Weighing from 165.8 to 173 grains, these *śalākā* coins, as they have been called, have been sometimes identified with the *śatamāna* of 100 *ratis*. Specimens of this coinage have been found in denominations of one-half, one-fourth, one-eighth, and one-sixteenth pieces. Other classes of coins of the same early type comprising (as they have been called) double and single *kārṣāpaṇas* have been found in deposits from western India and an unrecorded provenance in northern India.

To the same period as the Older Class of silver punch-marked coins as well as the bent bar coins belongs, if we are to judge from their simultaneous occurrence in the same Taxila deposit of circa 317 B.C., a group of minute silver coins with a single obverse mark and a blank reverse. They have been found not only on the site of Taxila, but also at Thathari in the Madhya Pradesh.

We have an interesting glimpse of the condition of the currency in northwestern India at the time of Alexander's invasion in the casual observation of a classical writer. We are told by Quintus Curtius that among the presents offered by the king of Taxila to Alexander were included thirty talents of *signatum argentum* ("coined silver"). We may identify these coins either with the Older Class of punch-marked coins or with the class of bent bar coins described above. The reference to silver coins in this connection, as R. B. Whitehead justly observes, probably signifies that silver was employed as the standard metal at that time. Of the currency conditions of the Maurya empire in Aśoka's last years, we have probably a valuable record in the shape of the Taxila hoard of punch-marked coins of the Later Class of circa 248 B.C., as above mentioned. These coins contain a considerable alloy of copper (75.3 per cent) as compared with the earlier silver coins (40.3 per cent) and in many cases are more than 54 grains in weight.

Turning to the subsidiary copper coinage of these times, we may mention that the class of square or rectangular cast coins bearing the characteristic symbols of "the hill and crescent," the hollow cross, and the like, has been held to have been issued by the Mauryas. To the same period has probably to be assigned a class of punch-marked copper coins with Maurya obverse marks, of which a hoard was found at Bhagalpur in 1925. With the Mauryas again we may probably connect numerous specimens of the remarkable copper coinage of Taxila, which extends over several centuries and is mostly uninscribed and die-struck. In a fragmentary stone plaque inscription of circa third century B.C., which was discovered some years ago at Mahasthan in the Bogra district of Bengal, reference is made to "a coin of the value of four cowries" called *gaṇḍaka.*

The downfall of the Maurya empire was not followed by the withdrawal of the imperial currency from circulation. From the finds of Indo-Greek coins in the same deposits at various sites, we may safely conclude that the punch-marked silver coins were in circulation down at least to the second and first centuries B.C. That their circulation was continued even down to the Kushān times is proved by a Mathurā stone pillar inscription of the twentieth year of Huvishka, mentioning an endowment of 11,000 *purāṇas.*

## Current and Forthcoming Asian Volumes in The Modern Nations in Historical Perspective Series of Spectrum Books

BUDDHIST LANDS OF SOUTHEAST ASIA by John F. Cady

CEYLON by S. Arasaratnam (Published 1964)

CHINA by Kenneth Scott Latourette (Published 1964)

INDIA by Stanley Wolpert

INDONESIA by J. D. Legge (Published 1965)

JAPAN by John W. Hall

MALAYSIA by John Bastin

PAKISTAN by A. R. Mallick

THE PHILIPPINES by Onofre D. Corpuz